Teach the Bairns to Bake

scones and bannocks, breads and baps, oatcakes, wee fancies, shortbreads and biscuits, tarts, gingerbreads, cakes, and sweets

Traditional Scottish Baking for Beginners

Liz Ashworth

illustrated by children from
Lhanbryde Primary School

Produced in Association with

of Speyside

Published in 1996 by
SCOTTISH CHILDREN'S PRESS
Unit 14, Leith Walk Business Centre,
130 Leith Walk, Edinburgh, EH6 5DT
Tel: 0131 555 5950
Fax: 0131 555 5018

In Association with Baxters of Speyside Ltd

Internal layout design: Avril Gray

SCOTTISH CHILDREN'S PRESS is an imprint of
Scottish Cultural Press

British Library Cataloguing in Publication Data
A catalogue record for this book is available from the British Library

ISBN: 1 899827 24 2

Printed and bound by Cromwell Press, Melksham, Wiltshire

Teach the Bairns to Bake is the second in an exciting new series of regional recipe books for beginners.

Also available:

Teach the Bairns to Cook
Traditional Scottish Recipes for Beginners
1 899827 23 4

Look out for further titles in the Children's Cooking series, including: Teagaisg Cocaireachd Dhan Chloinne (Teach the Children to Cook), Scottish Vegetarian Cooking . . .

Please contact SCOTTISH CHILDREN'S PRESS for further details or for a complete catalogue.

The Story of McChef

McChef has two pets: a cat called Lucy and a mouse called Samuel, who is rather grumpy but who loves eating McChef's food. McChef is very interested in Scottish cooking and hopes you will like his recipes as much as his pets do! McChef knows how important it is for us to learn how to cook good, wholesome food; a healthy body means a healthy mind too!

And ye shall eat in plenty, and be satisfied, and praise the name of the Lord your God, that hath dealt wondrously with you: and my people shall never be ashamed. (Joel 2: 26)

Contents

Foreword by Gordon Baxter, LL.D, OBE 4
Introduction 4

Important: Before you Begin to Bake 5
Lining Your Cake Tin 6
Preparing Trays, Tins and the Girdle 7
Mixing Methods and Testing Techniques 8
Dough and Dusting 9
Fruit Flavour 10
Easy Eggs 10
Simple Spoonfuls 11
Key 11
Handy Hints 12
Oven Temperatures and Baking Tips 13
Simple Baking Terms 14
Scones and Bannocks 15
Breads and Baps 31
Oatcakes 39
Wee Fancies 45
Shortbreads and Biscuits 51
Tarts 63
Gingerbreads 69
Cakes 77
Drinks 91
Jams, Marmalades and Preserves 99
Sweets 117

The Baxter Story 125
Bibliography 126
Index 127

Foreword

The Baxter family has resided in Fochabers for more than 250 years and I am proud that our company has been helped over the years by a growing band of loyal folk now numbering over 800. Our family company today creates an extensive variety of products made mainly from the superb natural produce of our own Highland area, and they are enjoyed in some 60 countries around the world.

During the 1970s, Liz Ashworth worked in our Product Development Department and then was the able manager of our Staff Canteen. Liz proved herself to be an original and creative cook with a gift for expressing her ideas simply yet imaginatively. Her first book, *Teach the Bairns to Cook*, filled a real need in the teaching of young folks the basic skills of cookery, diet and nutrition.

Now her second book, *Teach the Bairns to Bake*, shows young children the basic skills of baking such wonderful Scottish products as shortbread, bannocks, gingerbread and oatcakes. Older folk, too, will enjoy trying out these simple recipes.

I hope that this addition to Liz's series of books will bring pleasure to children and adults alike, both at school and in the home, and I am sure they will make their own special contribution to promoting our Scottish food-making traditions around the world.

Gordon Baxter, President
W. A. Baxter & Sons Ltd
November 1996

Introduction

The aim of this book is to help preserve our great Scottish baking tradition. By giving our children confidence and enjoyment making recipes and working in the kitchen, they will learn about, and pass on, this rich heritage of which we are rightly proud. Through the interesting stories associated with many of the recipes, I hope that *Teach the Bairns to Bake* will also give a picture of days gone by. Each recipe is graded simple, intermediate and advanced – and **it is intended that adults will always supervise children** making recipes which involve cooking or using sharp utensils.

Thank you to my mother who gave me a love of cooking at an early age. A special thank you to the late Mrs Doris Low, a wonderful cook, who gave me the benefit of her rich experience and knowledge. Thank you to Mr Gordon Baxter for his continued support, guidance and encouragement. He has helped in so many ways to make this exciting series of books. To Lhanbryde Primary School children, Mrs Allan the headmistress and her staff for their artistic contributions. To Janet Hall (a pupil at Elgin Academy) who has created McChef and his friends on the cover. Lastly, to my husband and son – my own personal guinea pigs!

Use this book to learn and to have fun with food. Good, wholesome food will help you to build a strong, healthy body and mind.

Liz Ashworth
November 1996

Important: Before You Begin to Bake

1) **Always** ask an adult for permission before you cook. If you are unsure or have never cooked on your own before do not be embarrassed to ask for help.
2) Decide on the recipe you would like to make and check how long it will take. Always read the recipe carefully right through before you start. Make sure you understand everything you have to do. Read through the list of ingredients and utensils again and set out everything you will need on the table before you start preparing the dish.
3) Arrange the shelves in the oven to the position indicated in the recipe before you turn on the oven to heat at the required temperature. (When you are using the oven, it is more economical to plan ahead and make a few things at the same time. Bake the recipe which needs the hottest temperature first.)
4) Always use a chopping board to chop food. Never hold a knife by its blade.
5) Have a heat-resistant surface nearby to set hot tins and baking trays on. A wooden chopping board will do.
6) A minute timer will make sure that the timing of your recipes is accurate. It will help you to remember your baking while you are tidying up afterwards!
7) Weigh all the ingredients very carefully – this is a very important part of successful baking. If you do not have kitchen scales, you can buy inexpensive measuring spoons and scoops from hardware shops which will help you to measure the quantities easily and accurately.
8) Wash and dry your hands, and all work surfaces, before you start.
9) For safety in the kitchen:
   - Tie back long hair.
   - Wear an apron or overall.
   - Do not wear open shoes or sandals in case of spills.
   - When you are stirring, mixing or beating, put a clean, damp cloth under the bowl to stop it from slipping.
   - Use oven gloves or mitts on both hands to lift hot trays, dishes, tins or pans.
   - Be careful with pans and girdles on the hob. Turn the handles inwards so that they can't be knocked off the hob. Be careful that handles do not overhang the hot hob. Always hold the handle of a pan when you are stirring or turning scones or pancakes.
10) Remember to turn off the oven, hob, gas or electricity when you have finished using it.

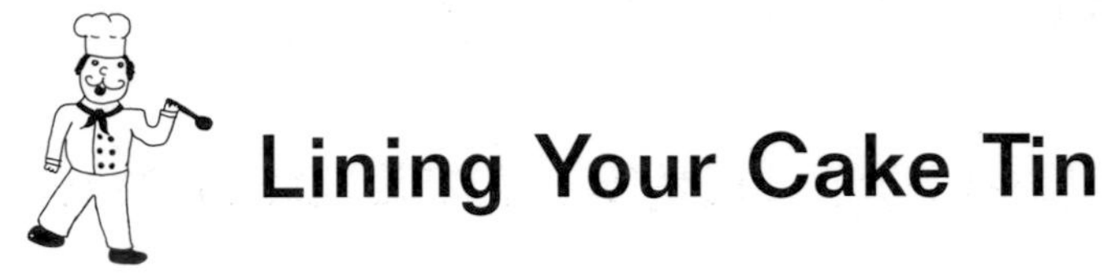

Lining Your Cake Tin

It is important to prepare cake tins before you make your cake. A properly lined cake tin gives the cake a good shape and helps it come out of the tin. You will need: vegetable oil, a pastry brush, a pencil, scissors and a roll of greaseproof paper. I used to love this bit when I was a little girl.

1) Lay the tin flat on the paper and draw round the bottom with the pencil. Do this again and cut out the two shapes you have drawn. These are for the bottom of the tin.
2) Now pull out the roll of paper flat on the worktop. Lay the tin on its side at the edge of the paper. Mark the depth of the tin on the paper with the pencil. Lift the tin and mark its depth again – you should have double the depth of the tin. Measure all round the tin and draw a strip which is long enough to go all round the tin with about 4cm (2 inches) extra.
3) Cut out the strip and fold it in half along its length to give a double thickness of paper the depth of the tin – this will go round the inside of the tin.
4) Take the folded end of the strip and make another fold about 1cm ($\frac{1}{2}$ inch) in from the edge. Use the scissors to make small diagonal cuts from the edge of the fold into this second fold all the way along.
5) Dip the pastry brush into some vegetable oil and carefully brush it all over the inside of the tin. Make sure that you get into all the corners.
6) Lay one of the bottom shapes into the base of the tin and brush with oil.
7) Carefully, making sure the slashed fold sits on the bottom, place the long strip round the inside of the tin. Push the paper against the side of the tin (it will stick to the oil) and gently press the strip to flatten it. Dip the brush in oil and carefully paint oil all over the paper in the tin.
8) Place the other bottom piece of paper on top of the slashed strip (it will stick to the oil), then paint it with oil too. Make sure that all the jagged edges are covered and the paper is not wrinkled.

Once you have had some practice this will be easy! It is very useful to know how to line a cake tin – it is especially important when you are making large, rich cakes as they need long, slow cooking and the lining protects them from drying out and tasting bitter.

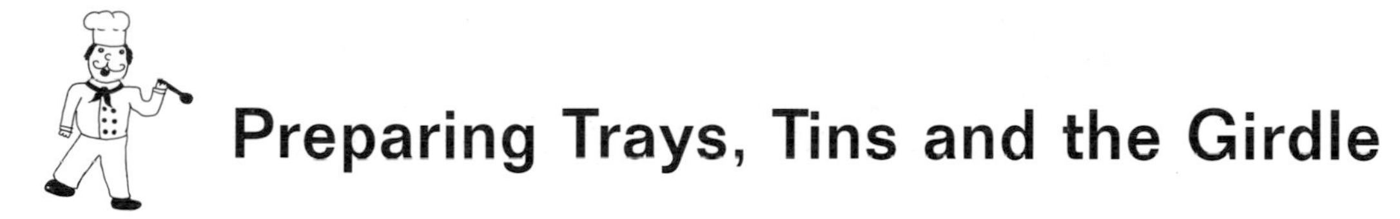

Preparing Trays, Tins and the Girdle

Oiling Baking Trays and Loaf Tins

Before you use a baking tray or loaf tin brush a little vegetable oil on it with a pastry brush. This stops your baking from sticking to the tray or tin – your baking comes out more easily and the tray won't need to be soaked before it is washed.

Lining Baking Trays and Loaf Tins

Some recipes ask you to line the baking tray or loaf tin.

1) Lay the tray on a sheet of greaseproof paper, draw round the base and cut out the shape.
2) Brush a little vegetable oil round the inside of the tin and stick the strip to the oil on the bottom of the tin.
3) Brush all over the paper with oil.

To Flour a Tin

This is important when baking sponges and bread mixtures.

1) Pour a little cooking oil into a cup and use a pastry brush to paint the oil all round the inside of the tin.
2) Put a teaspoon of flour into the tin and shake it all round the tin – it will stick to the oil. Make sure the inside is completely covered and then throw the rest of the flour away.

The Girdle

This is a thick, round iron plate with a half-hoop handle over the top. You can buy a girdle for use on modern cookers or you can use a thick-bottomed frying pan instead.

A new girdle has to be 'seasoned': do this by covering the surface with a thin layer of salt. Heat the girdle slowly until it is very hot, then leave to cool and remove the salt. Never wash the girdle; instead rub it with coarse salt and paper when it is cold and wipe it with a clean cloth. This builds up a non-stick surface.

Heating the Girdle

Put the girdle on to heat **before** mixing the scones so it is ready for the prepared scones.

To test: the girdle (or frying pan) is hot enough when a little flour sprinkled on the surface slowly turns brown. If it burns, the girdle is too hot and will need to cool a little.

Carefully dust off the flour. Grease the girdle or frying pan by rubbing a piece of cloth or kitchen paper dipped in cooking oil over the surface (this helps to stop your baking from sticking). Use oven gloves. You may need to do this again as you cook each batch. Remember the surface is hot – **always be very careful** when working with a girdle.

Mixing Methods and Testing Techniques

Rubbing In

This is one method of mixing fat (lard, butter or margarine) into flour. Cut the fat into small pieces and drop them into the flour in a bowl. Wash and dry your hands well. Mix the fat and flour together with your fingers: rub your thumbs along your fingers from your little finger towards your thumb gently rubbing the fat and flour between them. Lift your hands out of the mixture while you are rubbing, letting the fat and flour fall back into the bowl. Then drop your hands back into the bowl to get some more fat and flour.

Keep on doing this and after a few minutes you will see that the fat has disappeared and the mixture looks like fine breadcrumbs. Lifting the flour and fat out of the bowl traps more air into your mixture and helps to make your baking lighter.

Folding

Using a tablespoon, gently push into the mixture down and away from you, move the spoon through the mixture and then bring it up and out of the mixture towards you in a gentle circular motion. Repeat this until the ingredients are well mixed. This gentle method is used to keep as much air as possible in the mixture.

Beating

Stir the mixture very hard and quickly with a fork or whisk in a circular motion. This method is similar to folding but it is not so gentle and is much faster. Beating traps air in our baking which helps to make it rise and taste lighter.

Testing breads and cakes

Use a long skewer or needle to test breads and cakes to make sure they are cooked in the middle. To do this: use the oven gloves to take the tin from the oven. Push the skewer or needle into the middle of the loaf or cake. If the skewer comes out clean, the loaf or cake is ready. If there is still uncooked mixture sticking to the skewer, put the tin back in the oven for another 10 minutes and try again. Sometimes the top of the cake cooks more quickly than the middle. If the top is turning brown but the inside is not cooked, cover the cake with a double piece of greaseproof paper and reduce the oven temperature by 1 gas mark, 25°F or 10°C.

Scones and bannocks are ready when they sound hollow. **To test**: holding the scone with the oven gloves, carefully turn it upside down and knock on the bottom with the back of a spoon. If you are still unsure, try the cake test above. Scones which are not quite ready only need 3 to 4 minutes back in the oven or on the girdle.

Dough and Dusting

Doughs

Dough is made by mixing flour or meal with a liquid (like milk or water). The consistency or thickness depends on what you are making.

- Soft and pliable or elastic: the dough is like soft play dough which stretches easily. It is easy to pat or roll out. This dough is used for making scones and bannocks.
- Firm or stiff: the dough is much firmer and harder to mix and roll out. This mixture would be used for making biscuits.

Kneading Dough

Shake some flour over the worktop, rolling pin and your hands. Using both hands, push the dough down and away from you, squeezing it together. Still squeezing, pull the dough back towards you and then push it down and away again. Keep doing this until the dough is smooth and all mixed together.

Cutting Bread

An old cookery book advises that you 'cut new bread with a hot knife'. A handy tip is to slice all the loaf before you freeze it – then you can take the bread out slice by slice as you need it. You can easily separate the slices with a knife.

Shakers or Dredgers

You can buy shakers or dredgers from hardware stores; they look like a big mug with a lid on top which is full of holes – or you can make your own! Get a jam jar and carefully punch holes in the lid – make large holes for flour and small ones for sugar. Only put caster sugar in your sugar shaker – granulated is too rough and icing sugar is too fine.

Dusting Dough and Cakes

Dusting or shaking flour over the worktop, rolling pin and dough helps to stop it from sticking. Dusting sugar over cooked cakes or biscuits makes them look more attractive and adds to their sweetness. You should shake caster sugar on to shortbread or biscuits while they are still hot so that it will stick. Icing sugar must be dusted on when the cake or biscuit is cold, otherwise it will melt. To do this: put some icing sugar in a small sieve and shake it evenly over the cake or biscuit. You can lay a pretty doily on top of a cake and shake icing sugar over it – carefully remove the doily and you have pretty pattern!

Doilies are usually laid on plates before the cakes, scones or biscuits are laid on them. Dish papers, which are plain and have no cut-out decoration, are traditionally used under savouries such as sandwiches or buttered bread.

Fruit Flavour

Grating Citrus Rind

The rind is the shiny, firm, coloured, outer part of the skin of lemons, oranges and other citrus fruits. The white softer part underneath is called the pith and is bitter to taste.

1) Wash and dry the fruit well.
2) Place the grater on a large plate. Holding the grater in one hand, rub the skin of the fruit over the rough, dimpled part of the grater. Stop grating when the white pith appears.
3) Use the tip of a knife to scrape the rind off the grater on to the plate.

Squeezing Fruit Juice

You can remove the juice of lemons, oranges other citrus fruits with a lemon squeezer. Cut the fruit in half. Press and squeeze each half over the dome of the squeezer. The juice will collect in the surrounding channel while the stones are trapped in the little teeth which surround the dome.

If you do not have a squeezer, hold the cut fruit in one hand over a bowl, take a fork in your other hand and push it into the centre. Squeeze the fruit against the fork until all the juice has run out into the bowl. Use the prongs of the fork to remove any seeds which have fallen into the juice.

Easy Eggs

Breaking Eggs

Never break an egg directly into food in case it is bad. Hold the egg over a cup and tap the middle of the shell with a knife to crack it. Carefully, open the shell with your thumbs and let the inside of the egg drop into the cup. Check its smell and colour to see if the egg is fresh. If the recipe needs more than one egg, always break them into a cup one at a time and then add to a bowl for mixing. This means that you can throw out one which may not be fresh before it is mixed with the others.

To Separate Egg Yolk and White

An egg separator is like a small round flat cup with a slit in the side of it. Hold it over a bowl and break the egg into the cup; the egg white will run out of the slit into the bowl, leaving the egg yolk in the cup.

Another easy way to separate yolk and white: wash and dry the egg very carefully. Break the egg into a cup or bowl. Take half of the clean eggshell, carefully cut into the egg white with the sharp shell and lift out the yolk. Eggshell is more effective than a spoon because the sharpness of the shell cuts away the white sticking to the yolk and makes it easier to lift out. It is also perfect for lifting out any small broken pieces of eggshell.

Simple Spoonfuls

'Level' and 'Rounded'

Get a knife and smooth the amount on the top of the spoon so that it is flat – this is half a spoon and it is sometimes called 'a level spoon'.

One level teaspoon = half a teaspoon

One level tablespoon = ½ oz = 12.5g

When an amount of, say, flour is described as 'rounded', there is as much flour on the top of the spoon as the shape of the spoon below.

One rounded teaspoon = 1 teaspoonful

One rounded tablespoon of flour = 1oz = 25g

One tablespoon of liquid = 1 fl.oz = 25ml

Dessertspoon

A dessertspoon is a spoon which is bigger than a teaspoon but smaller than a tablespoon.

One tablespoon = 1oz

One dessertspoon = ½ oz

One teaspoon = ¼ oz

Key

Simple	Simple, straightforward recipe
Inter	Will require some help
Adv	Will need supervision and help throughout this recipe
1 hr 20 mins	The recipe will take one hour and 20 minutes to make (this time will change for each recipe)
Cook	Needs cooking
No Cook ☒	No cooking required
Hob ◎	Uses the hob
Grill ⌘	Uses the grill
Girdle ♉	A girdle may be used
E. Wok ❍	An electric wok may be used
E. Fry ❖	An electric frying pan may be used
Oven ☐	Uses the oven
Freeze ✳	Recipe may be frozen

Handy Hints

To Scrape a Bowl

Use a rubber spatula or bowl scraper to get all the mixture out of the bowl. A palette knife will do the job, too.

Cooling Your Baking

Rest your baking on a wire rack to cool. The holes in the wire allow the air to flow round the baking. This stops it from going soggy and at the same time helps it to cool. If you don't have a wire cooling rack, you can use the grid from a grill pan.

Butter or Margarine for Baking

When you are planning to make a recipe which asks for a 'creamed' mixture, take the butter or margarine out of the fridge to soften 30 minutes before you start to bake. This is not necessary for recipes where the fat is 'rubbed' in.

Treacle and Syrup

If you heat a spoon by standing it in a cup of very hot water for a minute before dipping it in the treacle or syrup you will find that the sticky treacle or syrup will run off the spoon easily. Heating the tin of syrup or treacle also helps, but do not heat it too much or it will become very runny.

1 level tablespoon of syrup or treacle = 25g = 1oz

Deep Fat

Test the temperature of deep fat by dropping in a piece of dry bread. If the bread bubbles and turns golden, the fat is ready. If the bread burns, the fat is too hot. If the fat does not bubble, it is too cold.

Buttermilk

Buttermilk is the liquid which is left after butter has been made from cream. Buttermilk is available from most supermarkets. It can be used instead of sweet (ordinary) milk but the raising agent in the recipe has to be altered as buttermilk contains more acid than sweet milk:

For every 275ml (½ pint) buttermilk add:
- 2 level teaspoons cream of tartar and
- 2 level teaspoons bicarbonate of soda

For every 275ml (½ pint) sweet milk add:
- 4 level teaspoons cream of tartar and
- 2 level teaspoons bicarbonate of soda

Pan Sizes

saucepan = a pan which holds 1½–2 pints (1.25l) of water

stew pan = a pan which holds 3–4 pints (2.5l) of water

large soup pot = a pan which holds 5–6 pints (3.5l) of water

preserving pan = a pan which holds 8 pints (4.5l) of water

Oven Temperatures and Baking Tips

Your Oven

Check whether your oven is gas or electric. An electric oven can be measured in two ways:

- If your oven shows a temperature range from 0° to 550°, it is measured in degrees Fahrenheit.
- If it shows a range from 0° to 250°, it is measured in degrees Celsius.

The temperature of a fan oven is higher than that of a conventional oven. You will need to decrease the baking temperature according to the manufacturer's instructions.

Be sure to read the recipe carefully and set your oven to the correct temperature.

Gas Mark			
1	275°F	140°C	low
2	300°F	150°C	
3	325°F	170°C	moderately low
4	350°F	180°F	moderate
5	375°F	190°C	
6	400°F	200°C	moderately hot
7	425°F	220°C	hot
8	450°F	230°C	very hot
9	475°F	240°C	

Oven Shelves

Different recipes are baked in different parts of the oven. Arrange the shelves for the recipe **before** you turn on the oven. If you need to re-arrange the shelves, use oven gloves.

If You Burn Yourself

- Call for an adult to come and help.
- If your skin is splashed with a hot liquid, or is touched by steam, or you accidentally touch a hot surface, put the affected area under cold running water as quickly as you can. This will take the heat out of the burn. You should keep it in the cold water for about 10 minutes.
- Remember, the quicker you get the burn into cold water the better chance you have of stopping it from blistering and causing scarring.
- You should be very careful around steam and boiling fat or oil. Steam and cooking fat are very hot, hotter than boiling water, and can give you a very nasty burn.

In Case of Fire

- Call an adult.
- Turn off the heat if it is safe to do so.
- Get away from the fire.
- Do NOT put water on it.

Simple Baking Terms

Batter A mix of flour, eggs and liquid. The thickness of the batter depends on what it is to be used for.

Beat To stir food fast. You can use a spoon, whisk or electric beater.

Boil To cook food over a high heat so that bubbles appear all over the liquid and steam rises from it.

Chop To cut food carefully into small pieces. To chop something finely is to cut it up as small as you can.

Cream To beat margarine or butter and sugar together until they are light in colour and fluffy in texture. This traps air and helps your baking to rise.

Egg Wash To paint the top of dough or pastry with beaten egg to give a golden, shiny top when baked.

Dice To cut food carefully into small, equal-sized cubes.

Drain To pour off the liquid which you don't need. You usually use a colander or a sieve which is placed over the sink.

Glaze To brush the top of dough or pastry with a mixture of milk or water and sugar to give a sweet, shiny top.

Grate To rub food against a grater so that the food is made into crumbs or fine shreds.

Grease To rub something with butter, margarine or oil. This stops food from sticking to it.

Pinch A pinch is the amount you can hold between your thumb and forefinger (pointing finger).

Prove To rise in a warm place before baking.

Sieve To rub flour and other dry ingredients through a sieve placed over a mixing bowl. Use the back of a tablespoon to push everything through the sieve. This removes lumps and adds air to your baking.

Simmer To cook food over a very low heat so that it bubbles now and then.

Slice To cut food into thin portions.

Sterilise To kill germs and bacteria. Sterilise jars and bottles by pouring boiling water into them, or place them in a hot oven for 15 minutes. (Use oven gloves.)

Stir To mix ingredients together with a spoon or fork until they are all well blended together.

Whip To beat a liquid with a whisk until it is light and frothy. Egg whites can be whipped until they are soft or until they form stiff peaks. **Do not over-beat egg whites** or they will become liquid and will never become light and fluffy again.

Scones and Bannocks

A bannock is a flat, round cake of dough – the size of a small plate – cooked on a girdle. A girdle is a large, flat, cast iron plate, with a half hoop handle over the top, which is heated over the fire. Originally, a hot, flat stone was placed beside the fire and used for baking. The girdle is heated, greased lightly with a little oil or butter and then the bannock is placed on the hot surface. When it has risen, the bannock is turned to brown on the other side before being lifted off the girdle on to a clean tea towel on a wire rack to keep warm and soft.

A scone is smaller than a bannock.The name comes from the Gaelic word *sgon*, meaning 'a shapeless mass' or 'a large mouthful'. Traditionally in Scotland scones and bannocks were eaten instead of yeasted bread and rolls.

Soda Scones

Scones were traditionally made using buttermilk.
Jugs of buttermilk used to be sold from carts in the streets of the cities and towns – it was called 'soor dook', and was a lot cheaper than milk.

Inter

16 scones
or 2 bannocks

25 mins

Cook

Hob

Girdle

E. Fry

Freeze

Have Ready

450g (1 lb) plain flour

2 level teaspoons bicarbonate of soda

2 teaspoon salt

275ml (½ pint) sweet milk

4 level teaspoons cream of tartar

(if you use buttermilk, you only need 2 level teaspoons cream of tartar)

girdle, frying pan or electric frying pan

mixing bowl

sieve

large plate

wooden spoon

tablespoon

teaspoon

palette knife

clean tea towel

wire cooling rack

oven gloves

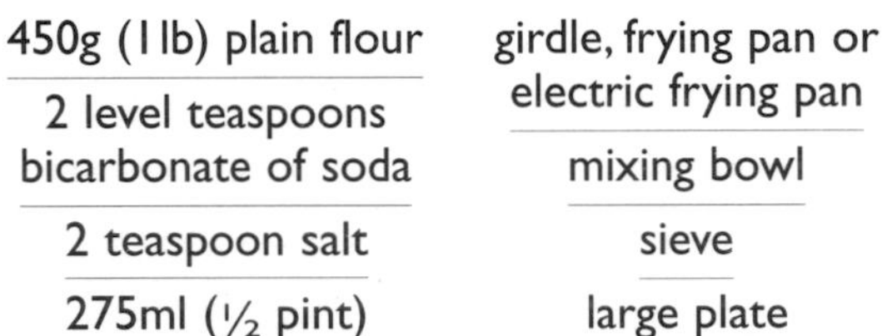

To Make

1 Put the girdle (or frying pan) on a medium heat.

2 Sieve the dry ingredients into the bowl.

3 Pour in the milk and mix with the wooden spoon to a soft dough. If the mixture is too stiff, add a little more milk.

4 Shake some flour over the worktop and scrape the dough on to the flour using the palette knife. Shake some flour over the dough and use the palette knife to cut it in half.

5 Rub some flour on your hands and shape each piece of dough into a round ball. Use the flat palm of your hand to press each ball into a round about 1cm (½ inch) thick.

6 Use the palette knife to cut the rounds in half, then into quarters then eighths. Shake some flour on the large plate and lift the scones on to the plate with the palette knife.

7 Test and grease the girdle (see page 7). Use the palette knife to place the scones on the girdle. Cook for 4 minutes on each side, turning with the palette knife, until golden. Tap the scones – if they sound hollow, they are ready.

8 Place the folded tea towel on the wire rack beside the hob.

9 Use the palette knife to place the scones inside the towel – this will keep them lovely and soft. Leave to cool a little and eat warm from the girdle with butter, cheese, jam, honey or syrup – have you any other ideas?

Mashlum Scones

When you use a mixture of different flours to make bannocks, it is called 'mashlum'. The bannocks made with this mixture are called 'Mashlum' or 'Meslin Bannocks' or 'Brash-bread'.

Inter

30 mins

Cook

Hob

Girdle

E. Fry

Freeze

Have Ready

- 110g (4oz) plain flour
- 110g (4oz) fine oatmeal
- 1 teaspoon cream of tartar
- 1 level teaspoon bicarbonate of soda
- 25g (1oz) margarine
- 150ml (¼ pint) buttermilk
- pinch of salt

- girdle, frying pan or electric frying pan
- mixing bowl
- sieve
- round scone cutter
- plate
- palette knife
- tablespoon
- teaspoon
- clean tea towel
- wire cooling rack
- oven gloves

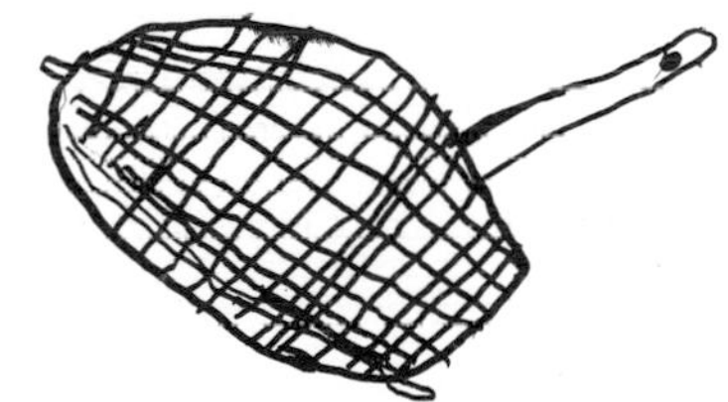

To Make

1. Put the girdle (or frying pan) on a medium heat.
2. Sieve the flour, cream of tartar, bicarbonate of soda and salt into the bowl. Add the oatmeal.
3. Cut the margarine into small pieces on the plate and add to the bowl. Rub the fat into the flour (see page 8).
4. Make a hollow in the centre of the mixture with the palette knife. Pour in the buttermilk. Mix to a soft dough using the palette knife. If the mixture is too stiff, add a little more milk.
5. Shake some flour on to the worktop and turn out the dough. Shake a little flour over the dough. Divide the mixture into 6 equal pieces using the palette knife.
6. Rub some flour on your hands. Gently and quickly shape the pieces into little balls. Use the palm of your hands to press them into flat, round cakes about 1cm (½ inch) thick.
7. Test and grease the girdle (see page 7). Shake a little flour on the surface of the girdle and use the palette knife to place the scones on the girdle. Bake for 4 minutes on each side, turning with the palette knife.
8. Lay the tea towel on the wire rack and use the palette knife to lift the scones on to it. Wrap them in the towel to keep them warm and moist. Mashlum Scones are best eaten the day they are made with butter and cheese.

Bere or Barley Bannocks

Inter

16 scones

30 mins

Cook

Hob

Girdle

E. Fry

Freeze

In the Highlands it was believed that kneading bannocks, stirring porridge or kail, even sending a drink round the table, must always be done in a clockwise or sunwise direction called 'deiseal'. This was thought to be lucky. To stir the opposite way, called 'widdershins', was believed to be unlucky.

Bere is a type of barley which is still grown in Orkney. It has a darker colour and a stronger flavour than barley and is a traditional ingredient in scones, bannocks and breads – especially in the Highlands, Orkney and Shetland. Beremeal and barleymeal or flour are available from health food shops and wholefood stores.

Have Ready

350g (12oz) barleymeal, barley flour or beremeal

330ml (3/4 pint) buttermilk

75g (3oz) plain flour

1 rounded teaspoon cream of tartar

1 rounded teaspoon bicarbonate of soda

1 teaspoon salt

girdle, frying pan or electric frying pan

large mixing bowl

sieve

palette knife

tablespoon

teaspoon

measuring jug

clean tea towel

wire cooling rack

oven gloves

To Make

1. Put the girdle (or frying pan) on a medium heat.
2. Sieve the flour, barleymeal, salt and cream of tartar into the bowl.
3. Measure the buttermilk into the jug and then stir in the bicarbonate of soda. When it froths up, pour it into the bowl and mix with the palette knife to make a soft dough.
4. Shake a little flour over the worktop and scrape the dough on to the flour using the palette knife. Shake some flour over the dough and use the palette knife to cut it in half.
5. Rub some flour on your hands and shape each piece of dough into a round ball. Use the flat palm of your hand to press each ball into a round about 1cm (1/2 inch) thick.
6. You can bake this bannock whole and cut it as required or cut each round into 6 or 8 scones with the palette knife.

7 Test and grease the girdle (see page 7). Use the palette knife to place the bannock or scones on the girdle, leaving enough room for the scones to rise and be turned easily with the palette knife.

8 Cook for 4 minutes on each side, turning with the palette knife, until golden on both sides. Tap the scones – if they sound hollow, they are ready. The bannocks will take a little longer to bake (5 to 6 minutes on each side).

9 Lay the clean tea towel on top of the wire rack and place it beside the hob.

10 Use the palette knife to lift the Bere Bannocks off the heat and wrap them in the tea towel. They are best eaten warm the day they are made. Bere Bannocks are delicious with home-made jam, honey or cheese. Try them as a snack with cheese and salad.

Samuel Johnson ate Bere Bannocks during a visit to Skye. Although the dark colour seemed a bit strange to him, he found that they were thick, soft and had an 'agreeable taste'.

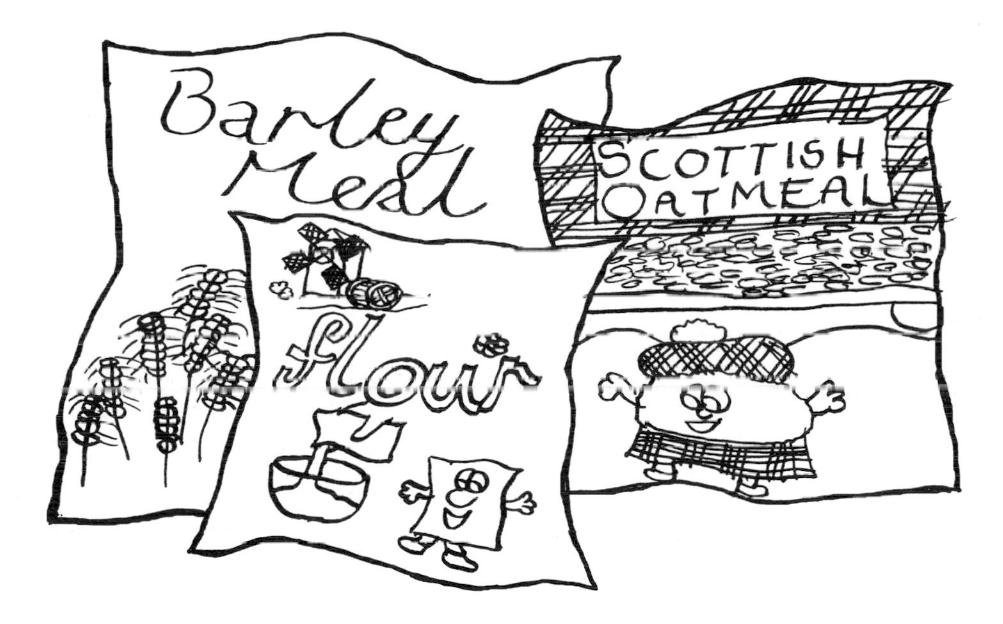

Fatty Cutties

Inter

8 cutties

30 mins

Cook

Hob

Girdle

E. Fry

Freeze

Fatty Cutties are a speciality of the Orkney Isles, where nearly all the baking was done on a girdle over the fire. They are similar to the traditional Welsh Cakes and Northumbrian 'Singin Hinnies'.

Have Ready

175g (6oz) plain flour

75g (3oz) granulated sugar

75g (3oz) currants

75g (3oz) butter or margarine

pinch of bicarbonate of soda

girdle, frying pan or electric frying pan

small pan

mixing bowl

sieve

palette knife

tablespoon

clean tea towel

wire cooling rack

oven gloves

To Make

1. Put the girdle (or frying pan) on a medium heat.
2. Sieve the flour and bicarbonate of soda into the mixing bowl. Add the currants and sugar and mix together.
3. Put the butter or margarine into the small pan and place on a low heat to melt. Turn off the heat.
4. Pour the melted butter or margarine into the bowl. Mix well with the wooden spoon to make a stiff dough.
5. Shake a little flour on the worktop. Turn the dough out on to the flour. Shake a little flour on top. Cut the dough in half with the palette knife.
6. Rub some flour on to your hands. Use the flat palm of your hands to shape and flatten each piece of dough into a circle about 0.5cm (¼ inch) thick.
7. Cut each circle into 4 triangles with the palette knife.
8. Test and grease the girdle (see page 7). Use the palette knife to place the Fatty Cutties on the girdle. Bake for 3 to 4 minutes, turning with the palette knife to brown both sides.
9. Place the folded tea towel on top of the wire rack. Use the palette knife to place the cooked cutties inside the towel. This will keep them soft and warm. Eat Fatty Cutties the day they are made – they taste really good when warm and newly baked!

Tattie or Potato Scones

Potatoes were not introduced to Scotland until 1700; however, it did not take long before they were adopted into a variety of recipes. Tattie Scones were usually made after the main meal when the left-over potatoes were still warm and soft.

Inter

20 mins

Cook

Hob

Girdle

E. Fry

Have Ready

225g (8oz) boiled, mashed potatoes

50g (2oz) flour

3 tablespoons milk

pinch of salt

girdle, frying pan or electric frying pan

mixing bowl

potato masher

wooden spoon

rolling pin

palette knife

plate

large round scone cutter

sharp knife

fork

clean tea towel

wire cooling rack

oven gloves

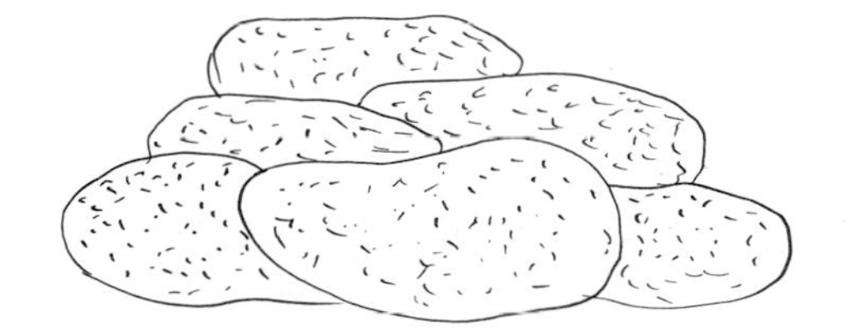

To Make

1 Put the girdle (or frying pan) on a medium heat.

2 Put the potatoes, milk and salt into the bowl and mash with the potato masher until they are smooth. Tap the potato masher on the side of the bowl to remove any mixture sticking to it.

3 Using the wooden spoon, start to beat the potatoes and add 1 tablespoonful flour. Mix well. Keep mixing in the flour 1 tablespoon at a time until the mixture is soft and smooth. If the dough is too stiff, add a little more milk.

4 Shake some flour over the worktop and turn out the dough. Shake some flour on top and rub flour on the rolling pin.

5 Use the rolling pin to roll out the dough to the thickness of a china plate. Cut into rounds using the scone cutter and prick the rounds all over with the fork. Lift the scones on to the plate and lay them beside the hob.

6 Test and grease the girdle (see page 7). Use the palette knife to place the scones on the girdle and bake for 3 to 4 minutes on each side, turning with the palette knife. The scones should be lightly browned on each side but still soft.

7 Lay the tea towel on the wire rack. Use the palette knife to lift the scones on to the towel. Wrap them up to keep warm. Traditionally, they were eaten hot, buttered and rolled up.

Mrs McNab's Scones

Inter

8 to 10 scones

30 mins

Cook

Oven ☐
8–10 mins

Gas 8, 450°F or 230°C

third shelf

Freeze ✳

Mrs McNab was a farmer's wife who lived in Ballater on Royal Deeside during the 1800s. She was an excellent baker and even royalty came to taste her recipes. Queen Victoria was said to have been especially fond of Mrs McNab's light scones.
The secret of the lightness of these scones is that the flour is sieved twice and they are handled as quickly and lightly as possible.

Have Ready

- 225g (8oz) self-raising flour
- 165ml (6 fl.oz) milk
- 25g (1oz) butter
- 1 egg
- 1 teaspoon cream of tartar
- ½ teaspoon bicarbonate of soda
- ½ teaspoon salt

- baking tray, floured *(see page 7)*
- 2 mixing bowls
- palette knife
- small bowl
- sieve
- knife + fork
- plate
- clean tea towel
- wire cooling rack
- oven gloves

To Make

1. Arrange the shelves and turn on the oven to heat.
2. Sift the flour and salt together into one bowl. Lift the sieve over the other bowl and sift the flour and salt through it again.
3. Cut the butter into small pieces on the plate and add to the flour. Rub the butter into the flour (see page 8).
4. Break the egg into the small bowl and beat it with the fork.
5. Use the palette knife to make a hollow in the middle of the flour mixture. Pour in the beaten egg and milk. Mix it all together to make a soft, elastic dough.
6. Shake flour over the worktop and turn out the scone dough, shake some flour on top and dust your hands with flour. Cut the dough into 8 or 10 equal pieces. Take each piece in your hands and quickly and gently make it into a little ball.
7. Put on the floured baking tray and press the top lightly with your palms.
8. Put the tray in the oven using the oven gloves and bake for 8 to 10 minutes until risen and golden brown on top.

9 Remove from the oven using the oven gloves. Use the palette knife to lift the scones off the tray and on to the wire rack to cool. Cover with the clean tea towel.

10 Eat the day they are made with butter and home-made strawberry jam (the recipe is on page 109) – mmmm! You will see why Queen Victoria liked these scones so much.

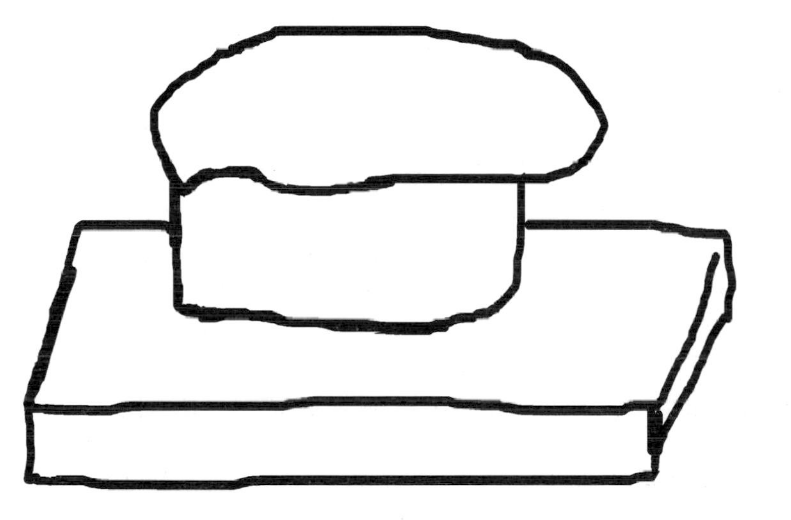

The Story of Wheaten Breads

Unleavened bannocks and scones were a staple, or common, food in Scotland and it was many centuries before yeasted or leavened wheaten bread became available to the ordinary working people. In the sixteenth century good quality, 'yeasted' wheaten bread was very expensive and only well-off people could afford this great luxury.

Four varieties of wheaten bread were made in Scotland during the sixteenth century.

Manche is a fine smooth bread. **Cheator Trencher** bread is coarser than Manche because it has some bran in the mix. **Ravelled** bread was baked with the ungraded flour from the mill which still contained the bran. After the bran had been sifted out of the flour (which was used to make finer bread) it was mixed with some rye to make **Mashloch**; a rough, cheap bread.

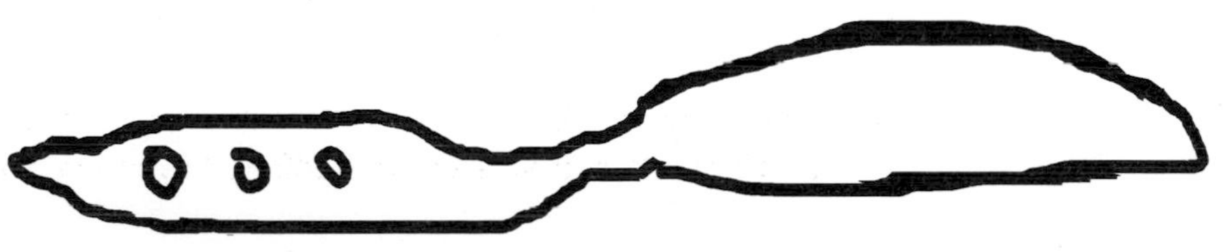

Sour Skons

Inter

Needs to soak for 2 days

9 skons

30 mins

Cook

Hob

Girdle

E. Fry

Freeze

This is another girdle-baked recipe from Orkney and Shetland. The oatmeal and buttermilk have to be soaked for 2 days – but it is well worth the effort to make these unusual sweet, caraway-flavoured scones.

Have Ready

- 110g (4oz) fine oatmeal
- 110g (4oz) flour
- 150ml (¼ pint) buttermilk
- 50g (2oz) caster sugar
- 1 teaspoon caraway seeds
- ½ teaspoon bicarbonate of soda

- girdle, frying pan or electric frying pan
- mixing bowl
- sieve
- wooden spoon
- tablespoon
- teaspoon
- palette knife
- clean tea towel
- wire cooling rack
- oven gloves

SOOR DOOK

BEST FRESH BUTTERMILK

To Make

Put the oatmeal and buttermilk into the mixing bowl and mix together. Cover and leave in a cool place for 2 days.

1. Put the girdle (or frying pan) on a medium heat.
2. Sieve the flour and bicarbonate of soda into the soaked oatmeal and buttermilk. Add the sugar and caraway seeds.
3. Mix together with the wooden spoon to make a soft, elastic dough. Add more buttermilk if the mixture is too stiff.
4. Shake a little flour on to the worktop and turn out the dough on to the flour. Shake some flour on top and rub some flour on your hands. Cut the dough in half with the palette knife. Take each piece of dough and gently and lightly shape into a round flat cake about 1cm (½ inch) thick. Cut into 4 triangles with the palette knife.
5. Test and grease the girdle (see page 7). Use the palette knife to place the skons on the girdle. Bake for 3 to 4 minutes each side, turning with the palette knife.
6. Fold the tea towel in half and lay on the cooling rack. Use the palette knife to place the skons inside the towel to keep them warm and soft.
7. Eat the skons the day they are made – they are delicious spread with butter. Caraway seeds have a flavour like aniseed and give Sour Skons a special taste which makes you ask for more!

Brunnies

The name for these thick bannocks from Orkney and Shetland comes from the Norwegian word for brown, brun. This recipe uses rye flour, which gives the Brunnies a very special flavour.

Inter

8 brunnies

30 mins

Cook

Hob

Girdle

E. Fry

Freeze

Have Ready

- 110g (4oz) wholewheat flour
- 110g (4oz) rye flour
- 1 tablespoon treacle
- 12g (½oz) butter
- 150ml (¼ pint) buttermilk
- 1 teaspoon cream of tartar
- 1 teaspoon bicarbonate of soda
- 1 teaspoon sugar
- generous pinch of salt

- girdle, frying pan or electric frying pan
- saucepan
- mixing bowl
- sieve
- palette knife
- wooden spoon
- tablespoon
- clean tea towel
- wire cooling rack
- oven gloves

To Make

1 Put the girdle (or frying pan) on a medium heat.

2 Sieve the flours, cream of tartar and bicarbonate of soda into the bowl – there will be small pieces of rougher grain left in the sieve, empty this into the bowl as well.

3 Put the butter and treacle in the pan and place on a low heat to melt the butter and soften the treacle – do not let them boil. Turn off the heat and pour the melted butter and treacle into the bowl.

4 Add the buttermilk and mix with the wooden spoon to a soft dough.

5 Shake some flour on the worktop. Turn the dough out on to the flour and shake a little flour on top. Rub some flour on your hands and shape the dough into a round, flat cake about 1cm (½ inch) thick. Cut into 8 triangles using the palette knife.

6 Test and grease the girdle (see page 7). Use the palette knife to place the Brunnies on the girdle. Bake for 4 to 5 minutes on each side until they are nice and brown.

7 Fold the tea towel in half and lay on the cooling rack. Use the palette knife to place the Brunnies inside the towel to keep them warm and soft. Brunnies taste wonderful warm with butter and cheese, jam, syrup or honey!

Dropped Scones

Inter

30 mins

Cook

Hob

Girdle

E. Fry

Freeze

These world-famous Scottish afternoon tea scones are made from flour, milk and eggs mixed to a batter which looks like thick cream. Dropped Scones are really a pancake and do not taste like a scone at all! The number of scones depends on the size of the spoon used to 'drop' them on the girdle.

Have Ready

- 225g (8oz) flour
- 4 level teaspoons baking powder
- 1 large egg
- 1 dessertspoon golden syrup
- 225ml (1½ gill) milk
- cooking oil

- girdle, frying pan or electric frying pan
- mixing bowl
- sieve
- measuring jug
- palette knife
- balloon whisk or wooden spoon
- tablespoon
- dessertspoon
- teacup
- knife
- clean tea towel
- wire cooling rack
- oven gloves

To Make

1. *Put the girdle (or frying pan) on a medium heat.*
2. *Sieve the flour and baking powder into the bowl.*
3. *Break the egg into the teacup.*
4. *Use the balloon whisk to make a hollow in the centre of the flour. Drop in the syrup and the egg.*
5. *Pour in the milk and whisk well. Do not be afraid to give the mixture a good beating to remove any lumps. The batter should be the thickness of thick cream – if it is too thick, beat in a little more milk.*
6. *Test and grease the girdle or frying pan* *(see page 7).*
7. *Lift out spoonfuls of the batter and drop them on to the girdle – leave a few centimetres between each scone. Use a tablespoon to make large scones, and a dessertspoon for smaller ones. You will see bubbles appear on top of the scone. When they burst, it is time to turn the scone.*
8. *Ease the blade of the palette knife underneath each scone and gently flip them over to cook the other side. Gently press the flat blade of the knife down on the cooked side of the scone – this pushes out any air trapped underneath and helps it to brown evenly.*

9 Fold the tea towel in half and lay it on the cooling rack.

10 Use the palette knife to place the scones inside the tea towel – the steam and warmth will keep them soft and spongy while you cook the rest of the scones.

11 Remember to oil the girdle after each batch. Watch the heat of the girdle – if the scones are pale and take a long time to cook, turn up the heat. If the scones brown too quickly on the outside and are still raw in the middle, reduce the heat.

It takes practice to make Dropped Scones but it is like learning to ride a bicycle – you never forget!

For sweeter scones, add more syrup; for thicker scones, make a thicker batter using less milk and cook at a lower temperature (thicker scones take longer to cook on each side).

Dropped Scones are best eaten as they are made – but let them cool a little first! Try them on their own or spread with butter, syrup, honey or jam – mmm! Do you have any original ideas?

The Story of Traditional Scottish Breads

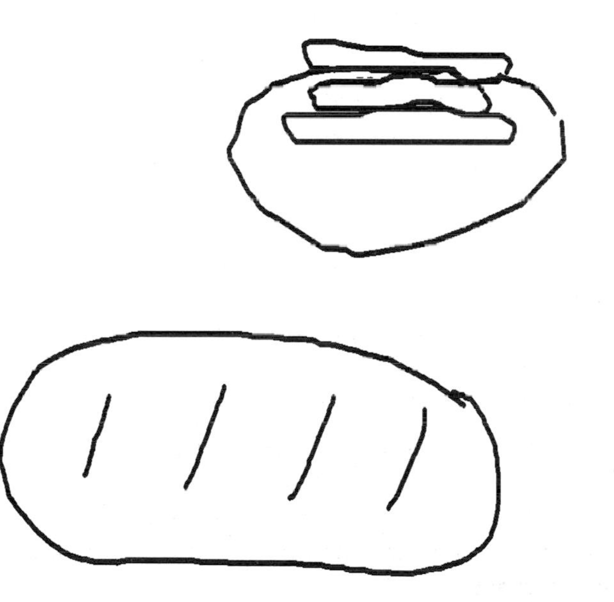

Different parts of Scotland had their own special breads and every baker had a different name for his particular bread. A **Soutar's Clod** is a rough, brown, yeasted wheaten bread with a thick clod-like crust. A very popular baker's shop in Edinburgh called 'The Baijen Hole' was well known for Soutar's Clods – they were quite large and were popular because of their good value.

An **Ankerstockn** is a large loaf made from rye flour mixed with currants and spices. It was sold at Hogmanay (New Year) as a special gingerbread. Today, Ankerstock gingerbread is still sold by bakers in Edinburgh. **Tod** or **Toddie** is a small round cake which was given to children to keep them happy. Although this bread was called 'Tod' or 'Toddie' in Roxburgh, it was 'Todgie' in Berwickshire and further north its name was 'Toly' or 'Toddle'. Have you ever heard of it? **Nacket** is a small loaf or cake of bread. It was eaten as a snack, usually at mid-day or with some wine. The custom comes from the border counties where it was called 'Nacket', 'Nockit' or 'Nackie'. **Snoddie** bread is traditional to Orkney. It is a thick, flat, round bread and is baked in the ashes of the fire.

Inter

Needs left overnight

30 mins

Cook ♒

Hob ◎

Girdle ♉

E. Fry ❖

Freeze ✳

Mealie Bannocks

This traditional Aberdeenshire version of Dropped Scones is made with oatmeal. The mixture has to be left to soak overnight to allow the oatmeal to soften and swell up (the oatmeal 'absorbs' the liquid).

Have Ready

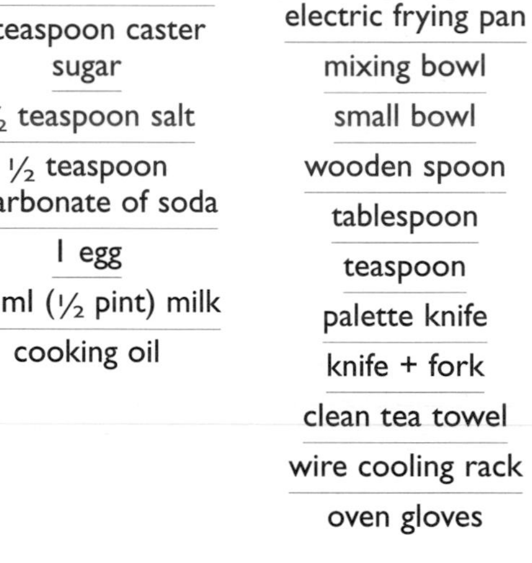

- 175g (6oz) oatmeal
- 1 teaspoon caster sugar
- ½ teaspoon salt
- ½ teaspoon bicarbonate of soda
- 1 egg
- 275ml (½ pint) milk
- cooking oil

- girdle, frying pan or electric frying pan
- mixing bowl
- small bowl
- wooden spoon
- tablespoon
- teaspoon
- palette knife
- knife + fork
- clean tea towel
- wire cooling rack
- oven gloves

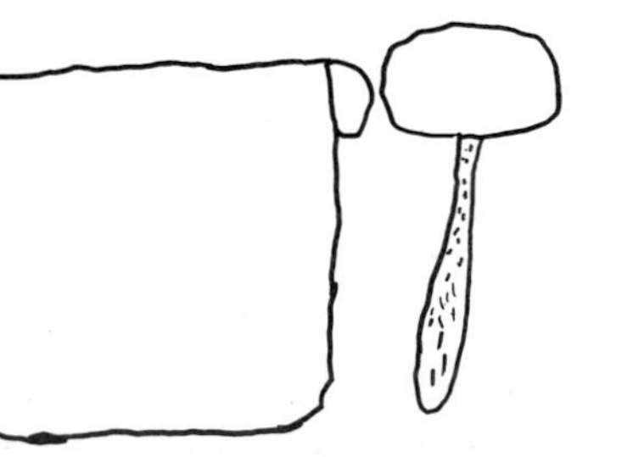

To Make

Put the oatmeal, sugar, salt and bicarbonate of soda in the bowl. Stir in the milk. Cover and leave in a cool place overnight.

1. Put the girdle (or frying pan) on a medium heat.
2. Break the egg into the small bowl and beat it with the fork. Add the egg to the oatmeal mixture and beat well with the wooden spoon. The mixture should be the thickness of double cream; add more milk if it is too thick.
3. Test and grease the girdle or frying pan (see page 7).
4. Drop tablespoons of the batter on to the girdle (use a dessertspoon to make smaller bannocks). Leave a few centimetres between each one. You will see bubbles appear on top, when they burst, it is time to turn the bannock.
5. Ease the blade of the palette knife underneath and flip each bannock over.
6. Gently press the flat blade of the palette knife down on the top of each bannock – this helps them to brown evenly.
7. Lift the bannocks off the girdle with the palette knife and pile them one on top of the other on the wire rack.
8. Cover with the clean tea towel. Mealie Bannocks taste best warm with butter and jam or syrup. Try them spread with cream cheese and jam on top – delicious!

Bride's Bonn or Bridal Cake

Bride's Bonn is traditional to Orkney and Shetland. As the bride walked into her new home for the first time as a married woman, it was the custom to break the whole bonn over her head!

Inter

30 mins

Cook

Hob

Girdle

E. Fry

Freeze

Have Ready

- 150g (5oz) flour
- 50g (2oz) butter
- 25g (1oz) caster sugar
- 1 teaspoon baking powder
- ½ teaspoon caraway seeds
- milk to mix

- girdle, frying pan or electric frying pan
- mixing bowl
- sieve
- plate
- wooden spoon
- tablespoon
- teaspoon
- teacup
- knife
- palette knife
- clean tea towel
- wire cooling rack
- oven gloves

To Make

1. Put the girdle (or frying pans) on a medium heat.
2. Sieve the flour and baking powder into the bowl.
3. Cut the butter into small pieces on the plate and add to the bowl. Rub the butter into the flour (see page 8).
4. Add the sugar and caraway seeds to the bowl.
5. Pour in half of a teacup of milk and mix together with the wooden spoon to give a soft dough. If the mixture is too dry, add more milk.
6. Sprinkle a little flour on to the worktop, turn out the dough and sprinkle with a little more flour. Rub some flour on your hands and shape the dough into a round, flat cake about 1 cm (½ inch) thick.
7. Test and grease the girdle or frying pan (see page 7). Lay the bonn on the girdle. Cook for 5 minutes on each side, turning with the palette knife. Use oven gloves to lift the bonn and knock on its bottom with your knuckles – if it sounds hollow, it is ready.
8. Place the tea towel over the cooling rack. Use oven gloves to lift the cooked bonn on to the towel and wrap it up.
9. Allow your bonn to cool before breaking it over a Bride's head!!! It is best to eat Bride's Bonn the day it is made.

Aberdeen Date Scones

This recipe comes from the city of Aberdeen, a seaport on the north-east of Scotland.

Inter

40 mins

1 large scone

Cook

Oven
20 mins

Gas 6, 400°F
or 200°C

middle shelf

Freeze

Have Ready

225g (8oz) flour

50g (2oz) chopped dates

25g (1oz) butter or margarine

1 egg

1 teacupful milk

1 dessertspoon syrup

1 teaspoon cream of tartar

½ teaspoon bicarbonate of soda

cooking oil

16cm (8″) oiled and floured sandwich tin *(see page 7)*

saucepan

mixing bowl

sieve

wooden spoon

tablespoon

dessertspoon

teaspoon

pastry brush

palette knife

plate

2 teacups

knife + fork

wire cooling rack

oven gloves

To Make

1. Arrange the shelves and turn on the oven to heat.
2. Sieve the flour, cream of tartar and bicarbonate of soda into the mixing bowl.
3. Cut the butter or margarine into small pieces on the plate. Add to the and rub into the flour (see page 8).
4. Break the egg into the teacup and beat it with the fork. Measure the milk into the other cup.
5. Put the syrup into the saucepan and place on a low heat to melt the syrup – do not let it boil. Pour into the bowl.
6. Add the chopped dates to the bowl. Pour in the milk and half the beaten egg. Mix well with the wooden spoon to make a soft dough. If it is too stiff, add a little more milk.
7. Use the palette knife to scrape the dough into the sandwich tin and smooth the top. Use the pastry brush to brush the remainder of the beaten egg over the top of the dough.
8. Use the oven gloves to put the tin in the oven. Bake for 20 minutes until the top is risen and golden brown.
9. Remove the tin from the oven using the oven gloves and set on the wire rack to cool in the tin.
10. When the scone is cool, tap the tin sharply on the worktop, loosen with the blade of the palette knife, turn the tin over and the scone will come out. Cut into 6 or 8 wedges. Eat on its own or spread with butter.

Breads and Baps

In 1773, when Dr Samuel Johnson and James Boswell toured the Highlands and Hebrides of Scotland, they were advised at Fort Augustus to carry bread with them on their journey northwards. The reason became clear when they stopped for some rest and food in Glensheals (the land of the clan Macrae). A woman brought them pails of milk to drink with their meal and as they ate they were watched by lots of wild-looking Highlanders and their families. Realising that the people were only curious and did not mean them any harm, James Boswell shared the remains of their bread with the onlookers and discovered that they had never seen a wheaten loaf before, let alone tasted one.

Dried yeasts, which are easier to use than fresh yeast, are now available. They can be added directly into the flour mix and the dough only needs to prove (rise) once. The amount of yeast you need is shown on the packet and is according to the weight of flour used in the recipe.

It is important to follow all the steps in a recipe carefully when you are cooking with yeast. Make sure that the kitchen and everything you use is warm. Cold draughts, mixing bowls or liquids can kill the action of the yeast – so can liquids which are too hot. Yeast mixtures are put into a hot oven to kill the action of the yeast and stop it working. If we did not do this, the yeast would continue to grow and the bread would have huge holes in it and be very tough to eat.

Butteries, Buttery Rowies or Aberdeen Rowies

Adv

16 rolls

3 hrs

Cook

Oven □
20 mins

Gas 6, 400°F
or 200°C

middle shelf

Rowies or Butteries are a traditional speciality of the North East of Scotland. They are very rich as they are made with layers of butter. They taste a bit like French croissants but they don't look like them! Once you have tasted a Rowie you will certainly want a second and even a third!

Have Ready

450g (1lb) strong white flour
225g (8oz) butter
110g (4oz) lard
1 tablespoon sugar
1 teaspoon salt
275ml (½ pint) tepid (barely warm) water
25g (1oz) fresh yeast (available from the bakers')

large baking tray
large mixing bowl
small bowl
sieve
rolling pin
wooden spoon
tablespoon
teaspoon
clingfilm
palette knife
wire cooling rack
oven gloves

To Make

1. Sieve the flour and salt into the mixing bowl.
2. Cream the yeast and sugar together in the small bowl. When it begins to bubble, add the tepid water.
3. Add the yeast mixture to the flour and mix together with the wooden spoon to make a soft, elastic dough.
4. Scrape the dough off the wooden spoon using the palette knife and then cover the bowl with a sheet of clingfilm.
5. Put the bowl into a warm place (with no cold draughts) and the dough will rise and double in size – this will take about 20 to 30 minutes.
6. Meanwhile wash and dry the small bowl and the wooden spoon.
7. Put the lard and butter into the small bowl and mix well with the wooden spoon. Use the palette knife to divide the mixture into three equal portions.
8. Shake a little flour over the worktop and check the dough. If it has doubled in size, remove the clingfilm and scrape the dough out of the bowl on to the floured top.
9. Shake some flour on top of the dough and over the rolling pin. Roll out the dough into a long strip about 1cm (½ inch) thick.

10 Take one portion of the fat mixture and use the palette knife to place little dots of fat all over the top of the dough.

11 Take one end of the dough strip and fold it over two thirds of the way. Then fold the other third on top to make a square. Leave the dough to rest for 10 minutes.

12 Arrange the shelves and turn on the oven to heat.

13 Roll out the dough again into a long strip and repeat steps 9, 10 and 11 twice more until all the fat is used. Remember to leave the dough to rest for 10 minutes after each rolling. (The dough needs to rest because the gluten, which makes flour elastic, is stretched a lot as it is rolled. If it is over-stretched, the dough will not rise properly and the rolls will be very tough.)

14 Divide the dough into 16 equal pieces using the palette knife.

15 Rub some flour on to your hands. Take each piece of dough in the palms of your hands and very gently and lightly shape into a ball. Place on the tray and gently flatten the top.

16 Cover the tray of dough balls with a sheet of clingfilm and leave to rise in a warm place for 30 minutes.

17 Remove the clingfilm and use the oven gloves to place the tray in the oven. Bake for 20 to 25 minutes until golden.

18 Use the oven gloves to remove from the oven. Lift the butteries off the tray with the palette knife and place on the cooling rack.

19 Butteries are best eaten warm with butter, marmalade, jam or cheese. They freeze very well so you can make them in advance, then you won't have to get up very, very early to make them for breakfast like they did a hundred years ago in your great-granny's time!

Baps (Scots Breakfast Rolls)

Inter

12 rolls

2 hrs

Cook

Oven
15 mins

Gas 6, 400°F
or 200°C

third shelf

Freeze

The grandfather of William Gladstone (1809–1898), Prime Minister of Great Britain, was the keeper of a small shop in Leith Walk, Edinburgh. He sold flour, oatmeal, dry goods and 'Baps'. He was known by the nickname of 'Sma Baps' because the baps he sold were smaller than those sold by the other shops nearby!

Have Ready

- 450g (1lb) flour
- 50g (2oz) lard or any white fat
- 275ml (½ pint) tepid milk and water mixed
- 25g (1oz) fresh yeast (available from the bakers')
- 1 teaspoon sugar
- 1 teaspoon salt

- baking tray, oiled
- mixing bowl
- small bowl
- sieve
- measuring jug
- palette knife
- wooden spoon
- pastry brush
- knife
- plate
- clingfilm
- tea towel
- wire cooling rack
- oven gloves

To Make

1. Fill the mixing bowl with warm water and leave it for a few minutes until the bowl is warm. Empty out the water and dry the bowl.
2. Sift in the flour and salt. Cut the lard into small pieces, add it to the bowl and use your fingers to rub it into the flour and salt.
3. Measure 150ml (¼ pint) of warm water into the measuring jug. Add enough milk to make 275ml (½ pint). Make sure that the temperature is just blood heat. Test by dipping a clean finger into the liquid. It should feel neither hot nor cold.
4. Put the yeast and sugar into the small bowl and cream together with the wooden spoon to make a paste. Add the tepid milk and water mixture and mix well.
5. Pour the yeast mixture into the flour and mix together to make a soft dough. Cover with clingfilm or a plate and leave to rise in a warm place for 1 hour.
6. Lightly oil the baking tray while you are waiting (see page 7).

7 When the dough has risen, shake a little flour on the worktop and then scrape the dough out on to the flour. Shake some flour on top of the dough and knead lightly for about 5 minutes until the dough is smooth.

8 Divide the dough into 12 pieces with the knife. take each piece in your hands and gently shape into ovals about 6cm (3 inches) long and 4cm (2 inches) wide. Lay them on the oiled baking tray.

9 Brush with water (this will give your baps a nice shine when they are cooked) and then leave in a warm place for 15 minutes to rise again.

10 Arrange the shelves and turn on the oven to heat.

11 Gently press your finger into the centre of each bap to prevent them from blistering while they are baking.

12 Use the oven gloves to place them in the oven and bake for 15 minutes.

13 Use the oven gloves to remove the tray from the oven. Lift the baps off the tray with the palette knife and place on the wire rack to cool a little before eating.

Traditionally, baps were only served at breakfast with butter and marmalade or cheese. Dr Johnson preferred to eat his baps with marmalade or jam and felt that eating them with cheese spoiled all the other good flavours!

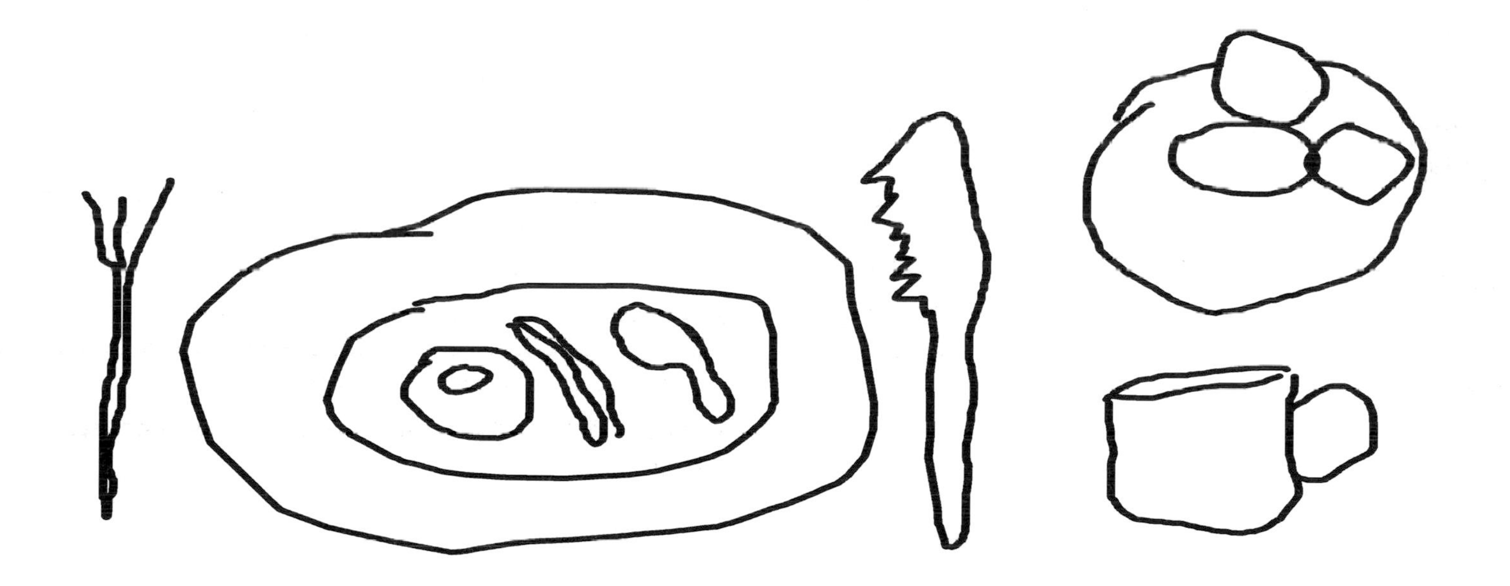

Buttermilk Bread

Inter

1 hr

Cook

Oven
35–40 mins

Gas 5, 375°F
or 190°C

middle shelf

Freeze

During the nineteenth and early parts of the twentieth century, housewives saved fuel by sending their half-baked bread and rolls to the bakers. They were allowed to bake them in the large ovens when the baker had finished baking his own batches of bread and rolls. At some bakeries you could even take your own flour and other ingredients and mix bread, sponges and cakes in the big mixers before baking them in the baker's ovens.

Have Ready

- 450g (1 lb) flour
- 25g (1 oz) sugar
- 25g (1 oz) butter
- 2 teaspoons bicarbonate of soda
- 2 teaspoon cream of tartar
- 1 teaspoon salt
- 275 ml (½ pint) buttermilk or sour milk

- baking tray, oiled *(see page 7)*
- mixing bowl
- measuring jug
- plate
- palette knife
- knife
- wooden spoon
- tablespoon
- teaspoon
- skewer
- wire cooling rack
- oven gloves

To Make

1. Arrange the shelves and turn on the oven to heat.
2. Sift the flour, bicarbonate of soda, cream of tartar and salt into the bowl.
3. Cut the butter into small pieces on the plate with the knife. Add to the bowl and then rub into the flour (see page 8).
4. Pour in the buttermilk and mix to a soft dough using the wooden spoon.
5. Shake a little flour on the worktop and turn the dough out on to the flour. Divide it into two with the palette knife. Shake some flour on the dough and shape both pieces into rounds. Place on the oiled tray and use the palette knife to cut across the top twice in an 'X' pattern.
6. Use the oven gloves to put the tray in the oven and bake for 30 minutes until risen and golden on top.
7. Remove the tray from the oven using oven gloves. Test the bread with a skewer and if it is ready loosen the bottom with the palette knife. Place the loaves on the wire rack – they will sound hollow when knocked on the bottom with a spoon.
8. Leave to cool and eat while it is fresh. Buttermilk Bread is lovely with butter, cheese and a salad.

To Make Bread Without Yeast

'It is a very impossible thing to get good yeast in the Highlands,' wrote Mrs Stuart of Arnesdale, Glen Quoich, in 1846. This recipe for bread without yeast comes from her cookery book and 'the same recipe with three parts of white flour and one of oatmeal makes a very good sort of "whitey brown" bread and is most strongly recommended to families who patronise Big Teas.'

Inter

1 hr

Cook

Oven
40–45 mins

Gas 4, 350°F or 180°C

middle shelf

Freeze

Have Ready

- 350g (12oz) flour
- 110g (4oz) fine oatmeal
- ½ pint buttermilk
- 2 level teaspoons bicarbonate of soda
- 2 level teaspoons cream of tartar
- 1 teaspoon salt

- 450g (1lb) loaf tin, lightly floured (see *page* 7)
- mixing bowl
- measuring jug
- palette knife
- wooden spoon
- tablespoon
- teaspoon
- skewer
- wire cooling rack
- oven gloves

To Make

1. *Arrange the shelves and turn on the oven to heat.*
2. *Sift the flour, bicarbonate of soda, cream of tartar and salt into the bowl.*
3. *Pour in the buttermilk and mix to a soft dough with the wooden spoon. Scrape the dough into the loaf tin with the palette knife and smooth the top.*
4. *Use the oven gloves to place the tin in the oven. Bake for 40 to 45 minutes until the bread has risen and is firm to the touch.*
5. *Use the oven gloves to remove the tin from the oven. Test it by sticking a skewer into the middle – if the skewer comes out wet, bake the bread for another 10 minutes.*
6. *Take the tin out of the oven with the oven gloves. Set it on the wire rack and leave to cool in the tin.*
7. *Wash and dry the palette knife. Loosen the sides of the loaf by all round the sides between the loaf and the tin. Remove the loaf from the tin while it is warm.*
8. *Eat on the day it is made – it is lovely with cheese or jam and is particularly good with lemon cheese (see recipe on page 116).*

Breakfast Baps (without yeast)

Often fresh yeast would not be available to make the rolls for breakfast – here is a recipe without yeast. These rolls are best eaten the day they are made.

Inter

8–12 rolls

30 mins

Cook

Oven ☐
12–15 mins

Gas 7, 425°F
or 220°C

third from top

Freeze

Have Ready

225g (8oz) flour

1 level teaspoon salt

25g (1oz) lard or white fat

3 level teaspoons baking powder

150ml (¼ pint) milk

baking tray, oiled *(see page 7)*

mixing bowl

measuring jug

sieve

wooden spoon

tablespoon

teaspoon

knife

wire cooling rack

oven gloves

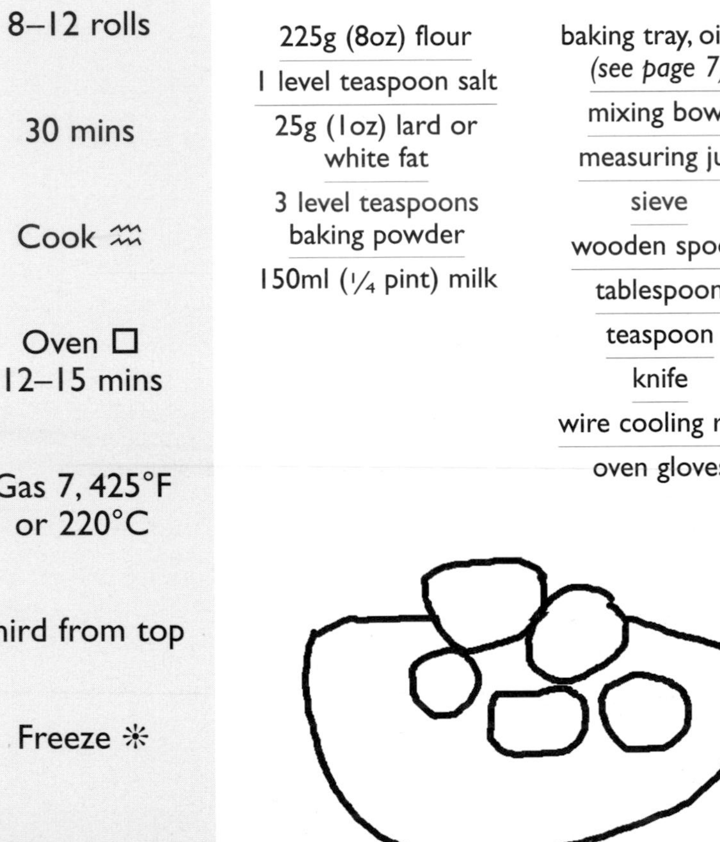

To Make

1. Arrange the shelves and turn on the oven to heat.
2. Sift the flour, salt and baking powder into the bowl.
3. Cut the lard into small pieces, add to the bowl and then rub into the flour (see page 8).
4. Measure the milk into the jug and pour into the bowl. Mix to a soft dough using the wooden spoon. Add more milk if the dough is too stiff.
5. Shake a little flour on to the worktop, scrape the dough on to the flour with the palette knife and then shake a little flour on top of the dough. Knead lightly for a minute and then roll into a fat sausage shape.
6. Decide how large you would like your rolls to be (remember they will rise in the oven). Use the knife to divide the dough into 8, 10 or 12 equal-sized pieces.
7. Rub some flour on your hands and gently shape the pieces into rounds. Place on the oiled tray and flatten slightly with the palm of your hand.
8. Put the tray in the oven using oven gloves. Bake for 12 to 15 minutes.
9. Use oven gloves to take the tray from the oven. Lift off the rolls with the palette knife and set them on the cooling rack. Eat warm with butter, jam, marmalade or cheese.

Oatcakes

Scotland is often called 'The Land o' Cakes' – not rich chocolate gateau or sticky toffee cakes, but oatcakes! Originally, the northern countries such as Scotland, Orkney and Shetland baked flat, unleavened cakes of bread on a girdle over the open fire. These were called 'kaaks'. In time, the kaaks of oatmeal became known as 'oatcakes'.

The first oatcakes were made of oatmeal and cold water mixed together. In the Hebridean islands off the west coast of Scotland, the fishermen made bannocks with handfuls of oatmeal mixed with seawater.

It was said that Scottish soldiers fed better and were fitter because they always carried a small bag of oatmeal with them. They would heat a metal plate in the fire and then mix some oatmeal and water into a dough which was shaped into a flat cake and 'baked' on the hot metal plate.

Oats and barley were the most widely grown grain, especially in Highland Scotland. Wheat was grown in the lowlands where the climate is milder, but the hardy oat was eaten all over Scotland. Oats are very good for you and are almost the perfect food, lacking only in Vitamin C which we get from eating fresh fruit and vegetables.

Fife Bannocks

Inter

8 farls

45 mins

Cook

Hob ◎

Girdle ♉

E. Fry ❖

Oven ☐
12–15 mins

Gas 5, 375°F
or 190°C

middle shelf

In the fertile Lowlands of Scotland more than one grain was grown, so cooks were able to mix some flour with the oatmeal and make an oatcake mixture which is much easier to handle. Try Fife Bannocks with honey fresh from the honeycomb.

Have Ready

175g (6oz) plain flour

110g (4oz) oatmeal

25g (1oz) butter or margarine

¾ teaspoon cream of tartar

½ teaspoon bicarbonate of soda

½ teaspoon salt

milk (use buttermilk if you have any)

girdle, frying pan, electric frying pan or baking tray

mixing bowl

rolling pin

sieve

plate

knife

tablespoon

teaspoon

palette knife

wire cooling rack

oven gloves

To Make

1. Put the girdle (or frying pan) on a medium heat or turn on the oven to heat.
2. Sieve the flour, bicarbonate of soda, cream of tartar and salt into the bowl. Add the oatmeal.
3. Cut the butter or margarine into small pieces on the plate. Add to the bowl and rub in with your fingers (see page 8).
4. Add 6 tablespoons of milk and mix well. Keep adding milk by the tablespoonful until you have a stiff but workable dough.
5. Shake a little flour on the worktop, scrape out the dough on to the flour using the palette knife and shake some more flour on top. Divide the dough into two equal pieces.
6. Flour the rolling pin. Shape one piece of dough into a round. Roll the dough and turn it, roll and turn until you have a thin circle of dough. Cut it into four. Repeat with the second piece.
7. Test and grease the girdle (see page 7). Use the palette knife to place the farls (see page 43) on the hot girdle. Cook until they are crisp and curled at the edges. Alternatively, put them on a baking tray, place in the oven and bake for 12 to 15 minutes until crisp.
8. Take them off the girdle with the palette knife and cool on the wire rack. Store in an airtight tin. Fife Bannocks are best eaten newly baked: they can be crisped in the oven for a few minutes if they become soft.

Bonnach Imeach

Bonnach Imeach is Gaelic for 'cake with butter'. This rich, thick oatcake comes from the Hebrides (islands off the West coast of Scotland). They taste best when they are freshly made – try them for lunch with cheese and fresh fruit or salad.

Inter

8 farls

35 mins

Cook

Hob

Girdle

E. Fry

Oven
15–20 mins

Gas 4, 350°F
or 180°C

middle shelf

Have Ready

225g (8oz) medium oatmeal

12.5g (½oz) butter

1 egg

4 tablespoons hot milk

½ level teaspoon salt

girdle, frying pan, electric frying pan or baking tray

mixing bowl

small pan

rolling pin

tablespoon

teaspoon

palette knife

plate

knife + fork

teacup

wire cooling rack

oven gloves

To Make

1. Put the girdle (or frying pan) on a medium heat or turn on the oven to heat.
2. Put the oatmeal and salt in the bowl. Cut the butter into small pieces on the plate and rub into the oatmeal (see page 8).
3. Pour the milk into the pan and warm it on a low heat.
4. Break the egg into the teacup and beat it with the fork.
5. Make a hollow in the oatmeal mixture and pour in the egg and milk. Use the palette knife to mix it all together and make a stiff dough.
6. Sprinkle a little oatmeal on the worktop and scrape the dough on to it. Sprinkle a little oatmeal on the dough and shape into a round with your hands. Roll the dough out with the rolling pin then turn it. Roll and turn in the same direction until you have an even round about 0.5cm (¼ inch) thick.
7. Cut the circle in half, then quarters, then eighths with the palette knife. Test and grease the girdle (see page 7).
8. Use the palette knife to put the farls (oatcakes) on the girdle. Bake for 4 to 5 minutes on each side. Alternatively, place on a baking tray and bake in the oven for 15 to 20 minutes.
9. Use the palette knife to set the farls on the wire rack to cool. Store in an airtight tin.

Traditional Highland Oatcakes

Inter

4 farls

30 mins

Cook

Hob

Girdle

E. Fry

Oven
12–15 mins

Gas 5, 375°F
or 190°C

middle shelf

A newspaper headline in 1745 could have been:
'Oatcakes helped our soldiers escape from Culloden Field.'

The battle of Culloden in 1745 was the last battle fought on British soil. It was between the English, led by the Duke of Cumberland, and the Jacobite army of Bonnie Prince Charlie (The Young Pretender). An old woman who lived in a cottage near the battlefield heard that the Scottish army was defeated. Quickly she carried her girdle, table and some oatmeal to the roadside. She lit a fire and baked oatcakes as fast as she could, laying them in a pile on the table. The soldiers grabbed an oatcake as they ran past fleeing to the hills for safety.

This dough becomes stiff and crumbly when left lying, so it is better to make one oatcake at a time, using the quantities given below. Prepare the next one while the first is baking. After baking on the girdle, the oatcakes really need to be crisped in the oven. However, if you don't have an oven, make sure that the oatcakes are well curled on the girdle and then cooled on a wire rack.

Have Ready

- 110g (4oz) fine or medium oatmeal
- 1 teaspoon lard, dripping or bacon fat (smoked bacon fat gives a lovely flavour)
- 150ml (¼ pint) hot water
- ½ teaspoon salt
- pinch of bicarbonate of soda

- girdle, frying pan or electric frying pan
- baking tray
- mixing bowl
- rolling pin
- palette knife
- large plate
- tablespoon
- teaspoon
- wire cooling rack
- oven gloves

To Make

1. Put the girdle (or frying pan) on a medium heat. Turn on the oven to heat.
2. Put the oatmeal, salt and bicarbonate of soda into the bowl. Make a hollow in the centre and add the fat.
3. Pour in enough hot water to mix to a stiff dough – you'll need about 150ml (¼ pint) but this will vary depending on the oatmeal used. Mix well with the wooden spoon.
4. Shake plenty of oatmeal on the worktop and use the palette knife to scrape the mixture on to it. Use your hands to form it into a smooth ball. Shake a little oatmeal over the top.
5. Oatcakes can be difficult to handle if they are allowed to cool as they start to crumble, so work quickly.

6 Roll three times across the ball to flatten it. Turn the dough round a quarter of a turn and roll again. Keep rolling and turning until you have a thin circle. Rub the top with oatmeal as you roll to prevent it from sticking and keep the edges as even as possible by pinching them with your thumb and forefinger.

7 Cut the round into quarters and put the oatcakes on the plate using the palette knife.

8 Test and grease the girdle (see page 7). Transfer the oatcakes (farls) from the plate to the girdle using the palette knife (carrying the oatcakes from the baking surface to the girdle on a plate helps to stop them breaking on the way!).

9 Cook until the edges curl up and oatcakes are dry and crisp.

10 Use the palette knife to lift them on to the baking tray. Use the oven gloves to place the tray in the oven for 3 to 4 minutes. The oatcakes may be dried under a warm grill for 1 to 2 minutes but watch them carefully as oatmeal burns very easily.

11 Remove the tray from the oven using the oven gloves and lift the farls on to the wire rack with the palette knife. Store in an airtight tin when cold. Spread your farls with butter and cheese or jam – they even taste good on their own. (You can heat the oatcakes in the oven for 4 minutes to re-crisp them if they become soft.)

The Story of Oatcakes

Each housewife had her own recipe for oatcakes, probably handed down to her through generations. Through years of practice, she knew how the dough should look and feel without having to weigh the ingredients. Specially made utensils were used to make the oatcakes: a stick called a 'spirtle' to stir the dough; a thin, small, notched kind of rolling pin called a 'bannock-stick; a long-handled 'spathe', almost like a heart shaped fish slice, lifted the oatcakes from the baking board on to a hot, flat, round metal plate or 'girdle' ('griddle') which hung over the fire and lastly a special rack called a 'banna-rack' was used to crisp the baked oatcakes. A bannock is the whole round oatcake. When it is cut into quarters they are called 'farls'. The cooled oatcakes were buried in the oatmeal in the meal-chest or 'girnel' to keep them fresh.

Oatmeal Cakes

Inter

12 oatcakes

45 mins

Cook

Oven
15–20 mins

Gas 4, 350°F
or 180°C

middle shelf

Many students at Scottish universities survived on a diet consisting mostly of oatmeal. They were given an official day's holiday every so often so that they could go back home to re-fill their oatmeal sack.

This recipe is for a sweet oatcake – it is more like biscuit than an oatcake. Try them with cheese and fruit or with a little home-made jam or lemon cheese.

Have Ready

- 1 teacup medium oatmeal
- 1 teacup plain flour
- ½ teacup milk
- 1 tablespoon soft brown sugar
- 75g (3oz) margarine
- 1 level teaspoon salt
- 1 level teaspoon bicarbonate of soda

- baking tray, oiled *(see page 7)*
- mixing bowl
- sieve
- rolling pin
- plate
- teacup
- tablespoon
- teaspoon
- palette knife
- large round scone cutter
- knife + fork
- wire cooling rack
- oven gloves

To Make

1. Arrange the shelves and turn on the oven to heat.
2. Sieve the flour, salt and bicarbonate of soda into the bowl. Add the oatmeal.
3. Cut the butter or margarine into small pieces on the plate. Add to the bowl and rub in with your fingers (see page 8).
4. Add the sugar and mix well.
5. Pour in the milk and mix to a stiff but workable dough using the palette knife. If it is too dry, add a little more milk.
6. Shake a little flour on the worktop and turn the dough out on to it. Shake a little flour on top and then roll out thinly (the thickness of a china plate). Prick all over with the fork.
7. Cut into rounds with the scone cutter and lay on the oiled baking tray.
8. Use the oven gloves to place the tray in the oven. Bake for 15 to 20 minutes until the biscuits are pale brown. Remove from the oven using the oven gloves.
9. Use the palette knife to lift the biscuits on to the wire cooling rack. Store in an airtight tin when cold. Robert Burns was very fond of oatcakes; he liked to eat them with a glass of ale.

Wee Fancies

Folk used to visit their *friends*, relations and neighbours a lot more than we do today – the upper classes spent most of their time travelling from one visit to the next! In her memoirs, Elizabeth Grant of Rothiemurcus describes the busy social life at her homes in Doune near Aviemore, in Edinburgh and in London. Mornings and afternoons were spent making visits where they were tempted with tea (or sometimes coffee), a wee dram of whisky and, of course, home-baking. She describes one particular visit to an old aunt, Lady Glenmoriston:

'I thought her cakes and custards excellent. My mother, who had seen them all come out of a cupboard in the bedroom, found her appetite fail her that morning!' (from *Memoirs of a Highland Lady, 1797–1827*)

Food was kept in some strange places because at that time people did not understand the need for hygienic storage.

Canmore Buns

This recipe is supposed to have originated at Cawdor Castle in Morayshire where Malcolm Canmore lived. He is the Scottish earl who killed Macbeth to become King of Scotland. He was called 'Canmore' because he had a large head.

Inter

18 fancies

45 mins

Cook

Oven
20 mins

Gas 4, 350°F or 180°C

middle shelf

Freeze

Have Ready

- 225g (8oz) flour
- 110g (4oz) butter or margarine
- 50g (2oz) caster sugar
- 50g (2oz) raisins (you can use currants, peel or sultanas instead of raisins)
- 1 level teaspoon bicarbonate of soda
- 1 teaspoon cream of tartar
- 1 egg
- 4 tablespoons milk

- baking tray, oiled and floured
- mixing bowl
- sieve
- plate
- teacup
- wooden spoon
- tablespoon
- teaspoon
- palette knife
- knife + fork
- wire cooling rack
- oven gloves

To Make

1. Arrange the shelves and turn on the oven to heat. Oil and flour the baking tray (see page 7).
2. Sieve the flour, bicarbonate of soda and cream of tartar into the bowl.
3. Cut the butter into small pieces on the plate, add to the flour mixture and rub in (see page 8).
4. Add the fruit and sugar and mix with the wooden spoon.
5. Break the egg into the cup. Add the milk, beat together with the fork and pour the mixture into the bowl.
6. Mix to a stiff dough – add more milk if it is too dry.
7. Rub a little flour on your hands and gather all the dough together in the bowl. Using the knife, cut the dough into 18 equal-sized pieces.
8. Take each piece and roll into a ball in your hands. Put them on the baking tray, leaving about 5cm (2 inches) between the buns to allow them to spread and rise.
9. Use oven gloves to put the tray in the oven. Bake for 20 minutes. Remove the tray from the oven using oven gloves and lift on to the wire rack with the palette knife. When they are cool, split your Canmore Buns and spread them with butter – yummy!

Sair Heidies

This recipe comes from the North East of Scotland.
Sair Heidies, or 'Sore Heads', are plain sponge cakes baked in straight paper cases which represent bandages. Sugar was crushed on top to represent aspirins!
A simple way to make straight-sided cakes is to bake them in muffin tins using muffin cases.

Have Ready

150g (5oz) flour
50g (2oz) margarine
50g (2oz) caster sugar
2 eggs
2 level teaspoons baking powder
crushed lump sugar

muffin tin or individual yorkshire pudding tray
pkt muffin cases
mixing bowl
small bowl
sieve
rolling pin
wooden spoon
tablespoon
2 teaspoons
teacup
fork
thick polythene bag
wire cooling rack
oven gloves

To Make

1 Arrange the shelves and turn on the oven to heat.
2 Put 8 muffin cases into the muffin tins.
3 Break each egg into the teacup, pour into the small bowl and beat together with the fork.
4 Put the margarine and sugar into the mixing bowl and beat well with the wooden spoon.
5 Pour in the eggs, sieve in the flour and baking powder and mix them well together.
6 Lift out a teaspoon of mixture and use the back of the other teaspoon to push it off the spoon into a muffin case. Half fill each case.
7 To crush the lump sugar: put some in a thick polythene bag and bash it with a rolling pin or the back of a wooden spoon.
8 Sprinkle a little crushed lump sugar on top of each cake. Use the oven gloves to place the tray in the oven and bake for 15 minutes until risen and firm.
9 Remove the tray from the oven with the oven gloves. Set it on a heat-resistant surface to cool a little and then lift the cakes on to the wire rack to cool. Enjoy your Sair Heidies!

Inter

45 mins

Cook

Oven
15 mins

Gas 5, 375°F or 190°C

middle shelf

Freeze

Aberdeen Crulla

Adv

12 fancies

1 hr

Cook

Hob

Freeze

These plaited, doughnut-like cakes come from the city of Aberdeen on the north-east coast of Scotland. At one time there was a strong Dutch connection with the city and in fact some people think the name 'Crulla' comes from a Dutch word, *krullen*, which means a curl or a scroll. Another theory is that 'Crulla' comes from the Gaelic word, *kril*, meaning 'a small cake'.

Have Ready

- 50g (2oz) butter
- 50g (2oz) sugar
- 150ml (1/4 pint) buttermilk
- 2 eggs
- 225g (8oz) flour
- 1 teaspoon baking powder
- 1 level teaspoon salt
- deep oil for frying
- caster sugar

- deep fat frying pan or deep fat fryer
- 2 baking trays
- mixing bowl
- small bowl
- tongs
- sieve
- teacup
- wooden spoon
- draining spoon
- teaspoon
- knife + fork
- measuring jug
- greaseproof paper
- kitchen towel
- serving plate + doily
- oven gloves

To Make

1. Pour the oil into the deep fat fryer and put on a low heat.
2. Put the butter and sugar in the mixing bowl and cream together with the wooden spoon.
3. Break each egg into the teacup and pour into the small bowl. Add the buttermilk and beat well with a fork.
4. Add to the butter and sugar and beat well with the wooden spoon.
5. Sift in the flour and stir to make a stiff dough – add more flour if it is too soft.
6. Shake a little flour on to the worktop, turn the the dough out on to the flour and knead for 2 minutes (see page 9).
7. Divide the dough into 12 equal-sized pieces. Roll each piece into a sausage shape about 7cm (3 inches) long. Cut each roll lengthways into 3 equal strips, leaving them joined at one end. Plait the strips by lifting the strip at the right side over the middle then lift the left strip over the middle. Repeat until you get to the end of the roll. Seal the ends by damping them with a little water and pressing them together.

8 Cover one of the baking trays with kitchen towel and lay it beside the hob. Cover the other with a sheet of greaseproof paper and spread this with a layer of caster sugar. Put this tray beside the first.

9 Turn up the heat under the deep fryer to medium and test the oil with a piece of bread. Carefully lift the Crullas into the oil using the draining spoon, then stand back from the hot oil. Cook the Crullas until they are deep golden on both sides, turning once with the draining spoon.

10 Using the draining spoon, lift out the Crullas and place them on the kitchen towel to drain.

11 Use the tongs to lift the Crullas on to the caster sugar. Lift the sides of the greaseproof paper to cover them in sugar.

12 Place the sugar-coated Crullas on the doily on the serving plate. They are best eaten warm and newly cooked – they taste absolutely wonderful! (If you want a different flavour, try adding 1 level teaspoon of ginger or nutmeg into the flour.)

Melting Moments

Inter

8–10 fancies

Cook

Oven
10–12 mins

Gas 4, 375°F
or 180°C

middle shelf

Traditionally cakes were served for afternoon tea on a 'cake stand'. This was a metal or silver-plated stand which held three plates in a tower. The bottom plate held plain bread and butter or small sandwiches, the middle plate held scones and pancakes and the top plate held the cakes or 'Fancies' as they were called. You had to eat your way to the top – no cakes without first eating from the first two plates!

Have Ready

110g (4oz) cornflour
75g (3oz) butter
50g (2oz) caster sugar
1 egg
1 level teaspoon baking powder
1 teaspoon grated lemon rind
icing sugar

tray of patty tins
pkt paper cake cases
mixing bowl
sieve
small sieve
large plate
wooden spoon
tablespoon
2 teaspoons
bowl scraper
teacup
fork
wire cooling rack
oven gloves

To Make

1 Arrange the shelves and turn on the oven to heat.
2 Sieve the flour and baking powder on to the plate.
3 Put the butter and sugar in the mixing bowl and cream with the wooden spoon until light and fluffy. Add the lemon rind.
4 Break the egg into the teacup and beat with the fork.
5 Add 1 tablespoon of cornflour and half the egg to the mixing bowl and beat well. Add another tablespoon of cornflour and the rest of the egg. Beat well and stir in the rest of the cornflour.
6 Put 10 paper cases into the patty tins. Lift out a teaspoon of mixture and use the back of the other teaspoon to push it off the spoon into a paper case. Repeat until all the mixture is used.
7 Use the oven gloves to place the tray in the oven and bake for 10 minutes until firm and golden.
8 Remove the tray from the oven using oven gloves and set on a heat-resistant surface. When they have cooled a little, lift the cakes on to the cooling rack.
9 When they are cold, dust your Melting Moments with icing sugar and serve with afternoon tea.

Shortbreads and Biscuits

Scottish shortbreads are world famous and are especially eaten at Christmas time and New Year. Traditionally, the edges are 'crimped' – a pattern made by pinching the shortbread between the thumb and forefinger before it is cooked. In the days when people worshipped the sun, this pattern represented the sun's rays.

The three main ingredients in shortbread are flour, butter and sugar. The rich, creamy flavour of shortbread comes from the butter, although margarine is sometimes used instead. There are different ways of mixing these ingredients together:

(1) Creaming the butter or margarine and sugar together.
(2) Rubbing the butter into the flour and sugar.
(3) Melting the butter before it is added to the flour and sugar.

I'm sure you will find *all* the different types of shortbread delicious! After you have made your favourite kind, why not put some pieces in a tin, tie it with tartan ribbon and give it to someone as a *really* special present.

Traditional Plain Scots Shortbread

Adv

1 hr 10 mins

Cook

Oven
20–30 mins

Gas 4, 350°F
or 180°C

middle shelf

The traditional way of making shortbread is messy, but fun! The housewives did not use a bowl to mix the ingredients, but worked them together on the clean tabletop just using their hands. If you are good with plasticine or play dough you will love this recipe – make sure you help to clean up while the shortbread is baking! Remember to take the butter out of the fridge to soften for 15 minutes before you start.

Have Ready

110g (4oz) plain flour

110g (4oz) butter

50g (2oz) rice flour

50g (2oz) caster sugar

20cm (8″) oiled sponge tin

baking tray, oiled *(see page 7)*

palette knife

bowl

sieve

small fine sieve or sugar dredger

fork

wire cooling rack

oven gloves

To Make

1. Arrange the shelves and turn on the oven to heat.
2. Sieve the flour and rice flour into the bowl.
3. Make sure your hands and the worktop are clean. Make a pile of sugar and lay the butter beside it. Using your hands, begin working the butter into the sugar using a kneading action until they are all mixed. Don't lick your fingers!
4. Now make another pile of flour beside your sugar and butter pile and work the flour in little by little until you have a mixture like pastry.
5. Press the mixture into the oiled sponge tin and smooth the top with the palm of your hand.
6. Turn the tin upside down on to the oiled baking tray. Tap the bottom of the tin so that the shortbread falls out on to the tray.
7. Now make the sun's rays by pinching the edges of the round with your thumbs and forefingers.
8. Prick all over with the fork and mark into 8 triangles with the blade of the palette knife. Do not cut all the way through.

9 Use the oven gloves to place the tray in the oven. Bake for 20 to 30 minutes until pale golden brown and crisp.

10 To test the shortbread: remove the tray from the oven using the oven gloves, look at the colour and then gently tap the shortbread – especially in the centre – with the back of a spoon. It should feel firm and sound hollow and crisp. If don't think it is ready, put the tray back in the oven and check every five minutes.

11 While the shortbread is still hot, dust a little caster sugar over the top.

12 Use the palette knife or a fish slice to gently lift the shortbread off the tray on to the cooling rack.

13 Store in an airtight tin when cold. By the time you have cleaned the kitchen and yourself I am sure that you will be ready to try the shortbread and it will be ready for you!

Shortbread (simple recipe)

Scottish shortbread is traditionally eaten at the festive season – no Hogmanay party is complete without a plate of shortbread! Why not make your own this year?

Inter

1 hr

Cook

Oven
25–35 mins

Gas 3, 325°F
or 170°C

middle shelf

Have Ready

175g (6oz) flour
110g (4oz) butter (soft)
50g (2oz) caster sugar
25g (1oz) cornflour

baking tray, oiled (*see page* 7)
mixing bowl
sieve
rolling pin
medium-sized round cutter
wooden spoon
tablespoon
fork
small sieve or sugar shaker
palette knife
plastic bowl scraper
wire cooling rack
oven gloves

To Make

1. Arrange the shelves and turn on the oven to heat.
2. Put the butter in the mixing bowl, add the sugar and cream with the wooden spoon until the mixture is pale and creamy.
3. Sieve the flour and cornflour into the bowl and mix well with the wooden spoon. Use your hands to bring all the mixture together into a ball. Knead lightly to make sure it stays together.
4. Shake a little flour on the worktop and lift the dough out of the bowl on to the flour. Shake a little flour on top then roll out to roughly 0.5cm (¼ inch) thick. Pinch the edges as you roll to keep the dough together. Prick all over with the fork.
5. Cut into rounds with cutter.
6. Knead the scraps together, roll out again, prick and cut more biscuits. Do not use too much flour as you are rolling out the scraps as this will make the mixture very crumbly.
7. Carefully lift the shortbread on to the baking tray with the palette knife. Use the oven gloves to put the tray in the the oven and bake for 25 minutes.
8. Check the biscuits: if they are pale brown and crisp, they are ready. If they need longer baking, put them back in the oven and check every 5 minutes.

9. Take the tray out of the oven using the oven gloves. Set the tray on a heat-resistant surface and shake a little caster sugar over the top of the biscuits while they are still hot.
10. Use the palette knife to lift the biscuits on to the cooling rack. Store in an airtight tin when cold.

For a surprise, you can use animal-shaped cutters and give them an eye by sticking a currant or raisin into the shortbread before it is cooked.

Often shortbread was decorated with almonds, caraway or strips of lemon or orange peel before it was baked. Pitcaithly Bannock is an example – see the recipe on page 62.

The Story of 'Infar-cake' or 'Dreaming Bread'

This is a decorated shortbread which was made for special occasions.

An old Scottish custom was to break a decorated cake of shortbread over the bride's head as she entered her new home and this was called an 'Infar-cake' or 'Dreaming-Bread'. Young men and women were given pieces of the bread to put under their pillows and 'dream' on. The superstition was that you would dream of the one you would marry. It is thought to come from a Roman custom (*confarratio*) where the bride and groom ate a specially consecrated cake at their marriage ceremony.

Oat Shortbread

Inter

12–14 biscuits

1 hr

Cook

Oven
15–20 mins

Gas 4, 350°F
or 180°C

middle shelf

The original shortbread recipes used oatmeal; today flour, cornflour or rice flour are used instead. Porridge oats can be substituted for oatmeal and this recipe uses a mixture of porridge oats and flour. You will love these – they are a great favourite with my son, Alan. He expects his Grandmother to provide a never-ending supply!

Have Ready

110g (4oz) porridge oats

110g (4oz) flour

75g (3oz) caster sugar

63g (2½oz) margarine

50g (2oz) lard

1 teaspoon baking powder

vanilla essence

caster sugar

pinch salt

baking tray, oiled *(see page 7)*

mixing bowl

sieve

bowl scraper

wooden spoon

palette knife

rolling pin

small sieve or sugar shaker

fork

wire cooling rack

oven gloves

To Make

1. Arrange the shelves and turn on the oven to heat.
2. Put the margarine, lard and sugar into the bowl and cream with the wooden spoon until pale and fluffy.
3. Add the oats and sieve in the flour. Add 2 drops of vanilla essence. Stir well until everything is mixed. Use your hands to bring all the mixture together into a ball. Knead lightly.
4. Shake a little flour over the worktop. Turn out the dough and divide in half. Shape each half into a rectangle. Roll out to roughly 5cm (2 inches) wide and 0.5cm (¼ inch) thick. Pinch round the edges with your thumb and forefinger.
5. Prick the dough with the fork and cut into fingers 1cm (½ inch) wide with the palette knife.
6. Carefully slip the blade of the palette knife under the shortbread fingers and lift them on to the baking tray.
7. Use the oven gloves to place the tray in the oven. Bake for 20 minutes or until pale brown and crisp.
8. Remove from the oven using the oven gloves and set on a heat-resistant surface. Shake a little caster sugar over the shortbread while it is hot.
9. Carefully lift on to the cooling rack with the the palette knife. Store in an airtight tin when cold.

Balmoral Shortbread

Queen Victoria was very fond of this plain shortbread and is said to have eaten some almost every day! When this recipe was made for her, it was made in the traditional way: after mixing it by hand on a board, the shortbread was rolled thinly, cut into rounds and pricked three times, one mark behind the other. This was the way it was also made at Buckingham Palace.

Have Ready

175g (6oz) plain flour
110g (4oz) butter
50g (2oz) caster sugar
pinch of salt
caster sugar

baking tray, oiled
(*see page 7*)
mixing bowl
wooden spoon
palette knife
rolling pin
fork
small sieve or sugar shaker
medium-size round cutter
wire cooling rack
oven gloves

To Make

1 Arrange the shelves and turn on the oven to heat.

2 Put the butter in the mixing bowl, add the sugar and cream with the wooden spoon until the mixture is pale and creamy.

3 Sieve the flour and salt into the bowl and mix well with the wooden spoon.

4 Use your hands to bring all the mixture together into a ball.

5 Shake a little flour on the worktop. Set the dough on the flour and shake a little flour on top. Roll out to the thickness of a china plate with the rolling pin.

6 Cut the dough into rounds with the cutter – lay them on the baking tray as you cut. Use the fork to prick the centre of each round 3 times – one behind the other.

7 Place the tray in the oven using the oven gloves. Bake for 15 minutes until golden and crisp.

8 Use the oven gloves to remove the tray from the oven and put it on a heat-resistant surface. Dust the shortbread with caster sugar while it is still hot. Use the palette knife to lift the shortbread on to the wire rack to cool.

9 Store in an airtight container and you can be like Queen Victoria and enjoy a piece of her shortbread every day!

Inter

18 biscuits

45 mins

Cook

Oven ☐
15 mins

Gas 4, 350°F
or 180°C

middle shelf

Adv

50 mins

Cook

Oven
15 mins

Gas 4, 350°F or 180°C

middle shelf

Petticoat Tails

Petticoat Tail shortbread has been enjoyed in Scotland for over four hundred years. It is a speciality of Edinburgh and the Lothians and was a great favourite with Mary Queen of Scots. A light, thin and crispy shortbread with a characteristic shape, it is thought to have been named after the hooped petticoats worn by the ladies of the court at that time. Another explanation for its name is that it is a corruption of the French *petites gatelles*, which means 'little cakes'. I like the first idea best!

Have Ready

350g (12oz) flour

110g (4oz) butter

38g (1½oz) caster sugar

4 tablespoons milk

1 teaspoon caraway seeds (optional)

baking tray, lined and oiled

saucepan

mixing bowl

sieve

wooden spoon

tablespoon

teaspoon

rolling pin

palette knife

large plate

glass tumbler

fork

sharp knife

serving plate + doily

wire cooling rack

oven gloves

To Make

1. Arrange the shelves and turn on the oven to heat. Prepare the baking tray (see page 7).
2. Sieve the flour into the bowl and add the caraway seeds.
3. Pour the milk into the saucepan and add the butter. Set the pan on a low heat until the butter is melted. Turn off the heat.
4. Make a hollow in the middle of the flour. Pour in the melted butter and milk.
5. Add the sugar and mix everything well. Use your hands to bring all the mixture together into a ball.
6. Shake a little flour on the worktop. Put the dough on it and then shake some flour over the top. Roll out to 0.5cm (¼ inch) thick.
7. Lay the plate on the dough and cut round it with the sharp knife. Gently lift off the plate.
8. Turn the glass upside down and use its rim to cut a hole in the centre of the circle of dough. Carefully lift out the round centre using the blade of the palette knife.

9 Pinch round the outer edges of both circles with your thumb and forefinger to give a notched pattern.

10 Cut the large circle into eight equal triangles. Lay them on the baking tray with the centre circle. Prick all the pieces lightly with the fork.

11 Use the oven gloves to put the tray in the oven. Bake for 15 minutes until pale golden brown.

12 Remove the tray from the oven using the oven gloves and set on a heat-resistant surface. Dust the shortbread with caster sugar while it is still hot.

13 Use the palette knife to lift the shortbread on to the wire rack to cool.

14 Place a doily on a serving plate. Put the small circle of shortbread in the middle with the petticoat tails laid round about it in a circle – there you have your hooped petticoats!

Tantallon Cakes

Named after the ruined castle of Tantallon which is situated a few miles east of North Berwick, these are not in fact cakes but a type of shortbread which is almost a cake! It is traditional to cut these cakes using a cutter with a scalloped edge.

Inter

12–15 cakes

1 hr

Cook

Oven □ 30 mins

Gas 6, 400°F or 200°C

middle shelf

Have Ready

- 175g (6oz) flour
- 175g (6oz) rice flour
- 175g (6oz) butter
- 175g (6oz) caster sugar
- 25g (1oz) icing sugar
- 2 eggs
- grated rind of 1 lemon
- 1 level teaspoon bicarbonate of soda

- baking tray, oiled
- mixing bowl
- small bowl
- sieve
- rolling pin
- wooden spoon
- small round scone cutter (with a scalloped edge if possible)
- teacup
- fork
- large plate
- palette knife
- small sieve or sugar shaker
- wire cooling rack
- oven gloves

To Make

1. Arrange the shelves and turn on the oven to heat. Oil the baking tray (see page 7).
2. Sieve the flour and bicarbonate of soda on to the large plate.
3. Put the butter and sugar in the bowl and cream with the wooden spoon until pale and creamy.
4. Break the eggs into the teacup and then add them to the small bowl. Beat with the fork.
5. Pour half the beaten egg into the mixing bowl. Add half of the flour and beat with the wooden spoon. Add the rest of the egg and flour and beat well.
6. Beat in the lemon rind.
7. Use your hands to bring all the mixture together into a ball.
8. Shake a little flour on the worktop. Set the dough on the flour and shake a little flour on top. Roll out to 0.5cm (¼ inch) thick. Cut the dough into rounds with the cutter, laying them 5cm (2 inches) apart on the baking tray as you cut them.
9. Use the oven gloves to put the tray in the oven. Bake for 30 minutes.

10 Remove from the oven – use the oven gloves! – and set on the wire cooling rack.

11 Dust with icing sugar when cool, then use the palette knife to lift the cakes off the baking tray.

12 Store in an airtight container.

These cakes were very popular in Edinburgh during the nineteenth century – I am sure when you have tasted them they will be just as popular with you and your friends now!

Pitcaithly Bannock

Pitcaithly in Perthshire is where people used to come to 'take the waters'. One of the landladies there made this cake for her boarders and it became very popular.

Inter

1 large bannock

1 hr

Cook

Oven
30–35 mins

Gas 4, 350°F
or 180°C

middle shelf

Have Ready

- 175g (6oz) flour
- 110g (4oz) butter
- 75g (3oz) caster sugar
- 50g (2oz) rice flour
- 50g (2oz) chopped almonds
- 50g (2oz) chopped mixed peel

- 19cm (8″) oiled sponge tin
- baking tray, lined and oiled (*see page 7*)
- mixing bowl
- wooden spoon
- teaspoon
- palette knife
- fork
- sieve
- small sieve or sugar shaker
- wire cooling rack
- oven gloves

To Make

1. Arrange the shelves and turn on the oven to heat.
2. Put the butter and sugar into the mixing bowl and cream with the wooden spoon until the mixture is pale and creamy.
3. Sieve the flour into the bowl and add the chopped almonds and chopped peel. Mix well together.
4. Use your hands to bring all the mixture together into a ball.
5. Press the dough into the sponge tin, smooth the top then turn the tin upside down on to the baking tray. Tap the bottom so that the shortbread falls out on to the tray.
6. Pinch around the edge with your thumb and forefinger. Prick with the fork and mark into 8 triangles with the blade of the palette knife.
7. Use the oven gloves to put the tray in the oven. Bake for 30 to 35 minutes until firm and pale golden. Gently press the middle of the bannock with the back of the teaspoon, bake for 5 to 10 minutes if it is still soft.
8. Remove the tray from the oven with the oven gloves and dust the shortbread with caster sugar while it is still hot. Lift it on to the wire rack using the palette knife.
9. When it is cool, you can gently break it into the marked triangles. Store in an airtight container. You don't have to go to Pitcaithly to taste this delicious bannock – enjoy it now!

Tarts

One of the most famous traditional Scottish cookery books is *The Cook and Housewife's Manual* by Mistress Meg Dodds. She was a character invented by Sir Walter Scott who did a lot to preserve and further traditional Scottish cooking through his writing. The cookery book itself was written by Mrs Isobel Johnston who was the wife of an Edinburgh publisher. This book and *The Cookery Book* by Lady Clark of Tillypronie have helped to preserve many of our old recipes.

Sir Walter Scott was a native of the Borders – a rich farming area. The recipes which come from there make use of all the fresh farm produce typical of the region; tarts are particular specialities.

Border Tart

The original Border tart was made with dough from the weekly bread-making. This more modern version uses shortcrust pastry.

Inter

1 hr

Cook

Oven
30 mins

Gas 4, 350°F
or 180°C

middle shelf

Freeze

Have Ready

175g (6oz) ready-made shortcrust pastry

Filling

50g (2oz) butter

50g (2oz) caster sugar

2 eggs

37g (1½oz) flour

25g (1oz) ground almonds

2 tablespoons raspberry jam

12.5g (½oz) flaked almonds

icing sugar

20cm (8″) flan dish or tin, oiled *(see page 7)*

mixing bowl

small bowl

small sieve

rolling pin

bowl scraper

large plate

wooden spoon

tablespoon

teacup

fork

oven gloves

To Make

1. Arrange the shelves and turn on the oven to heat.
2. Shake a little flour on the rolling pin and worktop. Place the pastry on top of the flour and roll out to the thickness of a china plate.
3. Lift the pastry by rolling it round the rolling pin. Lift it over the flan tin, let the edge of the pastry fall over the side of the tin and gradually unroll it over the tin. Gently ease it into the tin by pushing it into the corners with your knuckles. Press the bottom and sides flat with your fingers.
4. Fold the extra pastry over the rim of the tin and trim off the by rolling over the top of the tin with the rolling pin. The extra pastry will fall off.
5. Collect the scraps and knead them into a ball. Roll it out and cut into strips about 1cm (½ inch) wide.
6. Sieve the flour on to the plate and add the ground almonds.
7. Put the butter and sugar in the bowl and beat together until light and fluffy.
8. Break the eggs into the cup and then pour into the small bowl. Beat with the fork.
9. Add the eggs, flour and almonds to the butter and sugar and beat well together.

10 Use the back of the tablespoon to spread the jam over the base of the pastry in the flan tin.

11 Spoon the filling on top of the jam and smooth out with the bowl scraper.

12 Arrange the pastry strips on top in a lattice or criss-cross design. Trim off any strips that go over the edge of the tart.

13 Use the oven gloves to put the tart in the oven and bake for 20 minutes.

14 Remove from the oven using the oven gloves and set on a heat-resistant surface. Place some icing sugar in the small sieve and dust over the top of the tart.

15 Put the tart back in the oven (remember to use oven gloves!) for a further 10 minutes.

16 Remove the tart from the oven using the oven gloves and set on a heat-resistant surface to cool.

17 Border Tart is delicious hot or cold – it is particularly good with fresh cream!

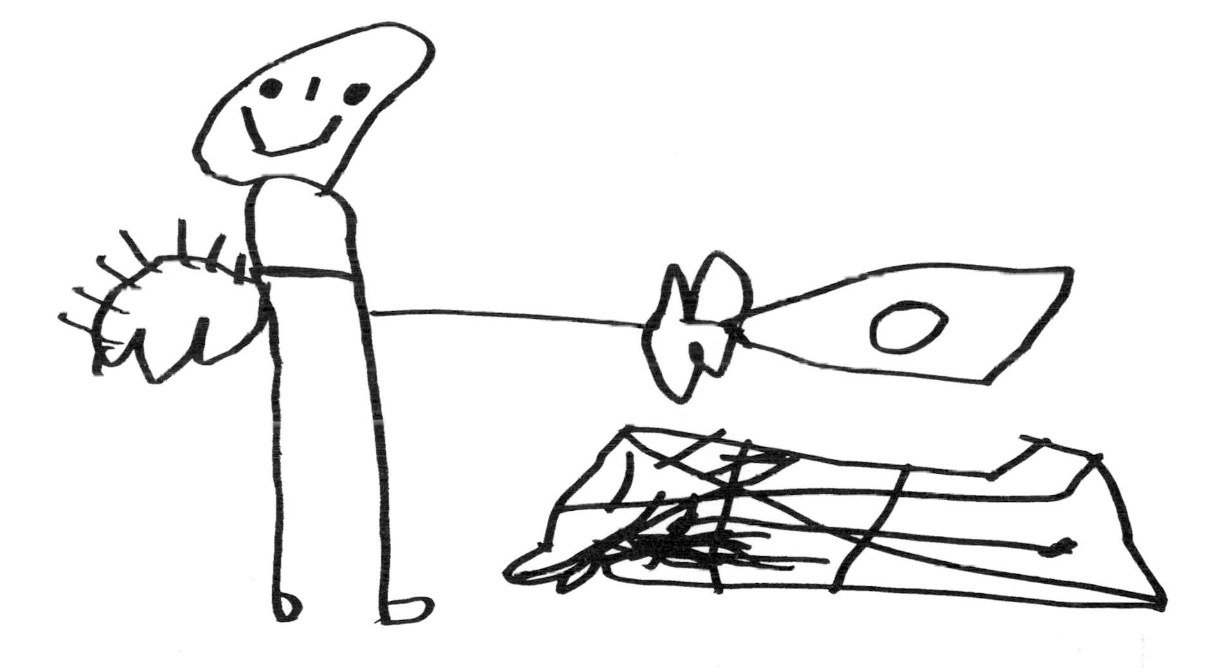

Eyemouth Tart

This is a version of Border Tart and is named after the fishing village of Eyemouth on the south-east coast of Scotland. This tart has a lovely crunchy texture and a sweet, tangy flavour – I'm sure you will love it!

Inter

1 hr 20 mins

Cook

Oven 25 mins

Gas 5, 375°F or 190°C

middle shelf

Freeze

Have Ready

175g (6oz) ready-made shortcrust pastry

Filling

- 75g (3oz) caster sugar
- 50g (2oz) chopped walnuts
- 50g (2oz) currants (or raisins)
- 50g (2oz) coconut
- 50g (2oz) chopped glace cherries
- 50g (2oz) butter
- 1 egg

Icing

- 50g (2oz) icing sugar
- lemon juice to mix

- 20cm (8") flan dish or tin, oiled *(see page 7)*
- saucepan
- mixing bowl
- small bowl
- rolling pin
- bowl scraper
- wooden spoon
- tablespoon
- dessertspoon
- teacup
- fork
- oven gloves

To Make

1. Arrange the shelves and turn on the oven to heat.
2. Follow steps 2, 3 and 4 for Border Tart (page 64) – lining the flan tin with pastry.
3. Melt the butter in the pan on a low heat. Turn off the heat.
4. Break the egg into the teacup and beat with the fork.
5. Put the walnuts, currants or raisins, coconut, cherries and sugar in the mixing bowl. Pour in the egg and melted butter and mix everything together with the wooden spoon.
6. Pour into the pastry case and level the top with the back of the bowl scraper.
7. Use the oven gloves to put the tin in the oven and bake for 25 minutes until evenly browned.
8. While the tart is baking, measure the icing sugar into the small bowl. Add 1 dessertspoon of lemon juice and mix well. Keep mixing in 1 teaspoon of lemon juice until the icing is a coating consistency – when it runs off the back of the spoon and leaves a smooth coating.
9. Use oven gloves to remove the tart from the oven. Set on a heat-resistant surface. Pour the lemon icing over the top and spread with the back of the dessertspoon dipped in hot water. Leave to cool, then cut into wedges to serve.

Ecclefechan Butter Tart

Ecclefechan is in the Border counties of Dumfries and Galloway. Traditionally, Ecclefechan Butter Tart was a small individual tart; it was really another variation of Border Tart.

Inter

1 hr 20 mins

Cook

Oven ☐
30 mins

Gas 5, 375°F or 190°C

middle shelf

Freeze

Have Ready

175g (6oz) ready-made shortcrust pastry

Filling

110g (4oz) mixed dried fruit

75g (3oz) soft brown sugar

50g (2oz) butter

1 egg

25g (1oz) chopped walnuts

1 dessertspoon wine vinegar

20cm (8″) flan dish or tin, oiled *(see page 7)*

saucepan

mixing bowl

rolling pin

bowl scraper

wooden spoon

teacup

fork

oven gloves

To Make

1. Arrange the shelves and turn on the oven to heat.
2. Follow steps 2, 3 and 4 for Border Tart (page 64) – lining the flan tin with pastry.
3. Break the egg into the teacup and beat with the fork.
4. Melt the butter in the pan on a medium heat. Turn off the heat.
5. Put the sugar into the mixing bowl, pour in the butter and beaten egg and mix together with the wooden spoon.
6. Add the vinegar, fruit and nuts and stir well.
7. Pour into the pastry-lined flan dish and level the top with the back of the bowl scraper.
8. Use the oven gloves to put the tin in the oven and bake for 25 to 30 minutes until golden.
9. Use oven gloves to remove the tart from the oven. Set it on a heat-resistant surface to cool. Ecclefechan Tart has a beautiful buttery flavour and tastes really good hot or cold – it is even better with cream or ice-cream.

Queen Mary's Tart or Edinburgh Tart

This is referred to as an 'Old Scots tea-table dainty' and was a great favourite of Mary Queen of Scots.

Inter

1 hr

Cook

Oven
30 mins

Gas 5, 375°F or 190°C

middle shelf

Have Ready

175g (6oz) ready-made shortcrust pastry

Filling

50g (2oz) butter

50g (2oz) caster sugar

50g (2oz) chopped mixed peel

2 eggs

1 dessertspoon raisins or sultanas

20cm (8″) flan dish or tin, oiled *(see page 7)*

saucepan

small bowl

teacup

fork

bowl scraper

wooden spoon

dessertspoon

oven gloves

To Make

1 *Arrange the shelves and turn on the oven to heat.*

2 *Follow steps 2, 3 and 4 for Border Tart (page 64) – lining the flan tin with pastry.*

3 *Break each egg into the teacup, pour into the bowl and beat with a fork.*

4 *Put the butter, sugar, chopped peel, sultanas or raisins in the pan. Place on a medium heat to melt the butter. Stir well and turn off the heat when the butter is melted.*

5 *Remove the pan from the heat, set on a heat-resistant surface and stir in the beaten eggs.*

6 *Pour the mixture into the pastry-lined flan dish and level the top with the back of the bowl scraper.*

7 *Use the oven gloves to put the tin in the oven and bake for 30 minutes until evenly browned.*

8 *Remove the tin from the oven using the oven gloves and set on a heat-resistant surface to cool.*

9 *Cut into wedges to serve. Queen Mary's Tart was traditionally served with afternoon tea – I'm sure you'd like to eat it anytime!.*

Gingerbreads

Long ago, housewives had certain days of the week for baking – one day for scones and another to make cakes and biscuits. They would bake enough for the whole week.

At the end of the nineteenth century High Tea became popular – it consisted of a hot savoury dish followed by bread, scones and jam, tea bread or cake, like gingerbread. It was not a grand meal and children usually 'filled up' with bread spread with jam. When visitors came, plates of cakes were laid on the table but the children were told, 'F. H. B.' (family hold back) – they had to leave the goodies for the visitors to have first choice!

Family life revolved around the kitchen. Large families, especially those living in very cramped conditions in the cities, often needed two sittings at mealtimes. Adults ate first and then the children. Conversation was encouraged but good manners were maintained with 'the wooden spoon'!

Parlies

Inter

I hr

Cook

Oven
30 mins

Gas 3, 325°F
or I60°C

middle shelf

Parlie is short for 'Parliament'. These cakes, which used to be sold from street stalls in Edinburgh, got their name because they were very popular with the members of the old Scottish Parliament. Although the recipe is similar to gingerbread, Parlies are in fact a delicious ginger treacle biscuit. The original recipe involves kneading *hot* dough with your hands – this is a simpler, safer version.

Have Ready

225g (8oz) flour

I I0g (4oz) soft brown sugar

I I0g (4oz) butter

I I0g (4oz) treacle

2 level teaspoons ground ginger

baking tray, oiled and floured (*see page 7*)

saucepan

mixing bowl

sieve

bowl scraper

palette knife

wooden spoon

tablespoon

dessertspoon

teaspoon

fork

wire cooling rack

oven gloves

To Make

1 Arrange the shelves and turn on the oven to heat.

2 Sieve the flour and ginger into the mixing bowl. Add the sugar.

3 Put the butter and treacle into the saucepan. Place the pan on a medium heat to melt the butter and treacle. (Be careful, this mixture is hot.) Turn off the heat.

4 Carefully pour the butter and treacle mixture into the bowl. Mix everything together with the wooden spoon.

5 Lay the oiled and floured baking tray beside the mixing bowl. Scoop up a dessertspoon of mixture and use the back of the teaspoon to push it off the spoon on to the tray. Repeat this leaving space between the biscuits to spread as they cook. Flatten each drop with the back of the fork.

6 Use the oven gloves to place the tray in the oven. Bake for 25 to 30 minutes. Remove from the oven (remember to use oven gloves) and use the palette knife to lift the biscuits off the tray on to the wire rack to cool and turn crisp.

7 Store your Parlies in an airtight tin – what a treat for your lunchbox!

Inverness Gingerbread

Around the year 1797, the Duchess of Gordon arranged what became known as 'the Northern Meeting' in Inverness. Once a year in the middle of October all the northern aristocracy gathered together and spent a week in Inverness. The mornings were spent visiting friends and enjoying the countryside, and in the evenings they attended dinners and balls. Perhaps they ate Inverness Gingerbread at their morning tea parties – it is quite likely as it was a popular cake even then.

Have Ready

- 350g (12oz) flour
- 350g (12oz) treacle
- 225g (8oz) butter
- 110g (4oz) fine oatmeal
- 110g (4oz) chopped candied lemon peel or mixed peel
- 25g (1oz) chopped candied ginger
- 4 tablespoons milk
- 1 teaspoon bicarbonate of soda

- 22cm (9″) square cake tin or 25cm (10″) round cake tin, oiled and lined *(see page 6)*
- saucepan
- 2 mixing bowls
- sieve
- bowl scraper
- wooden spoon
- tablespoon
- teaspoon
- skewer
- wire cooling rack
- oven gloves

To Make

1. Arrange the shelves and turn on the oven to heat.
2. Sieve the flour and bicarbonate of soda into a bowl. Add the oatmeal.
3. Spoon the treacle into the pan and put on a low heat to soften. Turn off the heat.
4. Put the butter into a bowl and beat with the wooden spoon until it is soft and creamy.
5. Beat in half the milk. Add half the flour and oatmeal and mix well. Beat in the rest of the milk, flour and oatmeal.
6. Add the treacle, chopped peel and ginger and beat well. Scrape the mixture into the tin using the bowl scraper.
7. Put the tin in the oven using the oven gloves and bake for 45 minutes. Test with a skewer or knife. If the gingerbread is wet in the middle, bake for a further 15 minutes.
8. Use the oven gloves to take the tin out of the oven and set on the wire rack. Leave to cool in the tin.
9. Remove from tin when cold and store in an airtight tin. Slice it thick and spread with butter – I bet gingerbread never tasted as nice as this!

Inter

1 hr

Cook

Oven ☐
45 mins to 1 hr

Gas 4, 350°F or 180°C

middle shelf

Freeze ✳

Orkney Broonie

Inter

1 hr 30 mins

Cook

Oven
1 hr 15 mins

Gas 4, 350°F
or 180°C

middle shelf

Freeze

This is an oatmeal gingerbread from Orkney. The name comes from the Norse word, *bruni*, which is a thick bannock. Orkney Broonie tastes best after it has been left in an airtight tin for a few days – see if you can leave it that long before you eat it!

Have Ready

- 175g (6oz) oatmeal
- 175g (6oz) flour
- 110g (4oz) soft brown sugar
- 50g (2oz) butter
- 275ml (½ pint) buttermilk (if available)
- 1 egg
- 2 tablespoons treacle
- 1 teaspoon ground ginger
- 1 level teaspoon bicarbonate of soda

- 900g (2lb) loaf tin, lined and oiled *(see page 7)*
- saucepan
- mixing bowl
- sieve
- bowl scraper
- measuring jug
- wooden spoon
- tablespoon
- teaspoon
- plate
- knife
- skewer
- wire cooling rack
- oven gloves

To Make

1. Arrange the shelves and turn on the oven to heat.
2. Sieve the flour into the mixing bowl and add the oatmeal.
3. Cut the butter into small pieces on the plate and add to the bowl. Rub it into the flour and oatmeal with your fingers (see page 8).
4. Add the ginger, bicarbonate of soda and sugar.
5. Put the treacle in the saucepan. Place on a low heat for the treacle to melt. Turn off the heat.
6. Break the egg into the cup and beat with the fork.
7. Pour the treacle, egg and buttermilk into the bowl and mix everything well together.
8. Pour the mixture into the prepared tin and use the oven gloves to put it in the oven. Bake for 1 hour.
9. Test with the skewer. If the cake is not ready, bake it for a further 15 minutes and repeat the test.
10. Remove the tin from the oven using oven gloves and set on the wire rack. Leave to cool in the tin. Store in an airtight tin for a few days before cutting. This rich, moist cake is lovely to eat on its own.

Fochabers Gingerbread

A recipe from the village of Fochabers in Morayshire. It is a very rich, expensive cake and is perfect for festive occasions.

Inter

2 hrs

Cook

Oven □
1 hr 30 mins

Gas 3, 325°F or 170°C

middle shelf

Freeze

Have Ready

- 450g (1 lb) flour
- 225g (8oz) butter
- 225g (8oz) treacle
- 110g (4oz) brown sugar
- 110g (4oz) sultanas
- 110g (4oz) currants
- 75g (3oz) ground almonds
- 75g (3oz) mixed peel
- 2 eggs
- ½ pint of beer
- 2 teaspoons mixed spice
- 1 teaspoon ground ginger
- 1 teaspoon ground cinnamon
- 1 teaspoon bicarbonate of soda
- ½ level teaspoon ground cloves

- 22cm (9″) square tin, lined and oiled *(see page 6)*
- saucepan
- large mixing bowl
- 3 small bowls
- measuring jug
- wooden spoon
- tablespoon
- teaspoon
- teacup
- fork
- bowl scraper
- skewer
- wire cooling rack
- oven gloves

To Make

1. Arrange the shelves and turn on the oven to heat.
2. Sieve the flour and spices into a small bowl.
3. Put the treacle in the pan and set on a low heat to soften. Turn off the heat.
4. Break each egg into the teacup and then pour into a small bowl. Beat with the fork.
5. Put the dried fruit and almonds into the other small bowl.
6. Put the butter and sugar into the large mixing bowl and beat with the wooden spoon until light and creamy. Pour in the treacle and mix well.
7. Pour in the eggs and beat well.
8. Add the flour and spices and mix well. Mix in the fruit.
9. Measure the beer in the jug and mix in the bicarbonate of soda. Pour into the mixing bowl and mix well together.
10. Use the bowl scraper to get all the mixture into the tin. Place in the oven (remember to use oven gloves) and bake for 1 hour 30 minutes. Test with a skewer. If still wet in the middle, bake a further 15 minutes.
11. Remove the tin from the oven using oven gloves and set on the wire rack to cool in the tin. When it is cold, cut into thick fingers.

Mrs MacLaren's Gingerbread

This is a simple recipe from an old Scots cookery book written in 1938 by Mrs MacLaren who was Head Mistress of the Girls' Technical School in Elgin. Her aims were to 'emphasise good nutrition by the good cooking of plain, wholesome food'.

Inter

1 hr 20 mins

Cook

Oven ☐ 1 hr

Gas 3, 325°F or 170°C

middle shelf

Freeze ✳

Have Ready

175g (6oz) flour

50g (2oz) soft brown sugar

50g (2oz) margarine

50g (2oz) treacle

25g (1oz) syrup

1 egg

150ml (1/4 pint) milk

1 teaspoon mixed spice

1 level teaspoon ground ginger

1 level teaspoon bicarbonate of soda

450g (1lb) loaf tin, lined and oiled

mixing bowl

saucepan

wooden spoon

tablespoon

teaspoon

teacup

bowl scraper

wire cooling rack

oven gloves

To Make

1. Arrange the shelves and turn on the oven to heat. Prepare the tin (see page 7).
2. Sieve the flour, bicarbonate of soda and spices into the bowl.
3. Break the egg into the teacup.
4. Put the treacle, syrup, sugar and margarine into the pan. Place on a medium heat to melt the margarine, stirring with the wooden spoon. Turn off the heat and pour into the bowl.
5. Pour in the egg and beat well with the wooden spoon.
6. Beat in the milk – the mixture will be like very thick pouring cream. Pour into the oiled and lined loaf tin.
7. Use the oven gloves to put the tin in the oven and bake for 1 hour. Test with a skewer.
8. Remove the tin from the oven using oven gloves and set on the wire rack to cool in the tin.
9. Take the gingerbread out of the tin when it is cold and store in an airtight tin. Mrs MacLaren's Gingerbread can be sliced and buttered and makes a good afternoon tea loaf. Try spreading it with some honey – lovely!

Black Piece

The original recipe for this cake required it to be baked in an oven pot – called a 'black pot'. This was an iron pot which was laid over a peat fire; peat embers were placed on the lid of the pot to brown the top of the cake inside.

Have Ready

- 225g (8oz) flour
- 50g (2oz) butter
- 50g (2oz) sugar
- 1 egg
- 2 tablespoons treacle
- 1 level teaspoon bicarbonate of soda
- 1 level teaspoon ground ginger
- 1 level teaspoon cinnamon
- 2 tablespoons warm water

- 450g (1 lb) loaf tin, lined and oiled
- saucepan
- mixing bowl
- sieve
- bowl scraper
- wooden spoon
- tablespoon
- teaspoon
- plate
- teacup
- knife + fork
- skewer
- wire cooling rack
- oven gloves

To Make

1. Arrange the shelves and turn on the oven to heat. Prepare the loaf tin (see page 7).
2. Sieve the flour, bicarbonate of soda, cinnamon and ginger into the bowl.
3. Cut the butter into small pieces on the plate, add it to the bowl and rub in with your fingers (see page 8).
4. Break the egg into the cup and beat with the fork.
5. Put the treacle in the pan and place on a medium heat to soften. Turn off the heat.
6. Add the treacle, egg and water to the bowl and mix well with the wooden spoon to make a soft mixture. Pour into the prepared loaf tin – use the bowl scraper to get all the mixture out of the bowl.
7. Use the oven gloves to put the tin in the oven. Bake for 45 minutes and test with a skewer.
8. Remove the tin from the oven using oven gloves. Set on the wire rack and leave to cool in the tin.
9. Take your Black Piece out of the tin when it is cold. Before you store it in an airtight container cut a thick slice and spread it with fresh butter – wonderful!

Inter

1 hr 15 mins

Cook

Oven 45 mins

Gas 4, 350°F or 180°C

middle shelf

Freeze

Edinburgh Gingerbread

Inter

2 hrs

Cook

Oven
1 hr 30 mins

Gas 3, 325°F
or 170°C

middle shelf

Freeze

In the *Memoirs of a Highland Lady, 1797–1827*, Elizabeth Grant of Rothiemurcus describes life in Edinburgh. She and her sister, Jane, often enjoyed dinner with their friends, the Jeffreys, at Craigcrook. 'Except in a real old-fashioned Scotch house, where no dish was attempted that was not national, the various abominations served up . . . were merely liables upon housekeeping.'

Have Ready

225g (8oz) flour
110g (4oz) butter
110g (4oz) treacle
110g (4oz) soft brown sugar
110g (4oz) chopped crystallised ginger
50g (2oz) raisins
50g (2oz) flaked almonds
2 eggs
2 level teaspoons ground cinnamon
2 level teaspoons mixed spice
2 level teaspoons ground ginger
1 level teaspoon ground cloves
1 level teaspoon bicarbonate of soda

18cm (7″) round cake tin, lined and oiled
2 mixing bowls
saucepan
small bowl
sieve
bowl scraper
wooden spoon
tablespoon
teaspoon
teacup
fork
wire cooling rack
oven gloves

To Make

1 Arrange the shelves and turn on the oven to heat. Prepare the cake tin (see page 6).

2 Put the butter, treacle and sugar in the pan. Place on a low heat to melt, stirring with the wooden spoon. (Be careful, this mixture is hot.) Turn off the heat.

3 Break each egg into the cup and then pour into the small bowl. Beat with the fork.

4 Weigh the dried fruits and nuts into a bowl.

5 Sieve the flour, spices and bicarbonate of soda into another bowl.

6 Pour the butter, treacle and sugar into the bowl of flour and spices. Add the beaten eggs and mix. Then add the fruits and nuts. Mix well with the wooden spoon.

7 Pour into the prepared tin and use the oven gloves to place it in the oven. Bake for 1 hour 30 minutes.

8 Remove from the oven using the oven gloves and test with a skewer. Set on the wire rack and leave to cool in the tin.

9 Cut your rich, fruity Edinburgh Gingerbread into thick slices and serve for a teatime treat!

Cakes

It was a long-established custom in Scotland to have a break from work about four o'clock in the afternoon – this break was known as 'the four-hours'. Originally, ale and claret were drunk at this time.

Tea was introduced to Scotland by Mary of Modena, the wife of James VII of Scotland and II of England, in 1681, when she and her husband stayed at Holyrood. To begin with, tea-drinking was denounced as sinful by the clergy, and the medical profession said it was bad for the health. It wasn't until the middle of the eighteenth century that tea became a common drink.

So 'the four-hour' became 'afternoon tea' and it became so popular in the nineteenth century that tea-rooms were built (one of the most famous in Scotland was Miss Cranston's Tea-Room in Glasgow).

Scotland has always been renowned for its delicious cakes. Dundee Cake, with its characteristic almond topping, and Black Bun, traditionally eaten at Christmas and Hogmanay (New Year), are world famous. But perhaps you haven't tried any of the other scrumptious Scottish cakes . . .

Scots Seed Cake

This cake has caraway seeds in it – they have an aniseed flavour and were used a lot to flavour cakes, scones and even shortbreads.

Adv

1 hr 30 mins

Cook

Oven
1 hr

Gas 4, 350°F or 180°C

middle shelf

Freeze

Have Ready

- 175g (6oz) flour
- 175g (6oz) butter
- 175g (6oz) caster sugar
- 3 eggs
- 50g (2oz) mixed peel
- 12g (½oz) caraway comfits
- 1 tablespoon brandy
- ½ level teaspoon nutmeg
- 1 level teaspoon caraway seeds

- 18cm (7″) round cake tin, lined and oiled *(see page 6)*
- large mixing bowl
- sieve
- skewer
- large plate
- 2 teacups
- small bowl
- bowl scraper
- fork
- wooden spoon
- tablespoon
- teaspoon
- whisk
- wire cooling rack
- oven gloves

To Make

1. Arrange the shelves and turn on the oven to heat.
2. Separate the egg yolks and whites (see page 10). Put the egg whites in the small bowl and whisk until they are frothy and form soft peaks (see page 14).
3. Sieve the flour on to the plate.
4. Cream the butter and sugar together in the mixing bowl.
5. Add 1 tablespoon of flour and 1 egg yolk then beat well. Repeat this until all the egg yolks have been added.
6. Stir in the mixed peel, nutmeg and caraway seeds.
7. Add the rest of the flour and the egg whites. Use the tablespoon to gently fold the ingredients together (see page 8).
8. Carefully stir in the brandy.
9. Spoon the mixture into the prepared tin and sprinkle the caraway comfits on top.
10. Use the oven gloves to place the tin in the oven and bake for 1 hour – watch that the top does not become too brown. If it does, lower the temperature to Gas 3, 325°F or 170°C and cover with a double sheet of greaseproof paper.
11. Remove from the oven using oven gloves and test with a skewer. Set on the wire rack to cool in the tin. Serve cut into thick wedges – a rich cake with a different flavour!

Snow Cake

This is a very old Scots family recipe for a light vanilla, lemon or almond flavoured cake – you can choose whichever flavour you like best!

Have Ready

225g (8oz) arrowroot

225g (8oz) butter

110g (4oz) caster sugar

3 egg whites

lemon, vanilla or almond essence

20cm (8″) round cake tin, lined and oiled *(see page 6)*

2 mixing bowls

electric whisk, beater or food mixer

tablespoon

wooden spoon

bowl scraper

wire cooling rack

oven gloves

To Make

1. *Arrange the shelves and turn on the oven to heat.*
2. *Using the wooden spoon, put the butter in a bowl and beat it until it is soft and creamy.*
3. *Sieve the arrowroot and sugar on to the plate. Gradually, one spoon at a time, beat them into the butter.*
4. *Separate the egg whites from the egg yolks (see page 10). Whisk the egg whites in a mixing bowl until they are stiff and stand up like mountain peaks.*
5. *Add the egg whites to the butter, arrowroot and sugar mixture. Beat with the electric whisk or food mixer for 15 minutes.*
6. *Add a few drops of your chosen flavour* (lemon, vanilla or almond essence) *and beat in.*
7. *Pour into the prepared tin and place in the oven (using the oven gloves) to bake for 1 hour.*
8. *Use the oven gloves to remove the tin from the oven – the cake will feel firm and springy when gently pressed with the back of a spoon. Test the centre with a skewer.*
9. *Cool in the tin on the wire rack and remove from the tin when cold. Snow Cake is best eaten soon after it is baked. Try some home-made jam or lemon cheese with it.*

Adv

1 hr 30 mins

Cook

Oven ☐
1 hr

Gas 4, 350°F
or 180°C

middle shelf

Freeze ✳

Scottish Strawberry Sandwich

This is a light cake with a taste of summer – the recipe comes from Aberdeenshire where folk obviously know how to make good use of the abundant local strawberries. When you produce this cake for tea everyone *will* be impressed!

Adv

40 mins

Cook

Oven □ 20 mins

Gas 4, 350°F or 180°C

middle shelf

Freeze (before filling)

Have Ready

- 110g (4oz) flour
- 110g (4oz) caster sugar
- 2 eggs
- 1 level teaspoon baking powder
- 3 tablespoons warm water

Filling

- 110g (4oz) strawberries
- 150ml (¼ pint) double cream
- 38g (1½oz) caster sugar
- 1 egg white
- vanilla essence

- 2 x 15cm (6″) sandwich tins, lined and oiled
- large pan
- mixing bowl
- 2 small bowls
- sieve
- whisk
- bowl scraper
- large plate
- palette knife
- pair tweezers
- teacup
- dish towel
- fork
- tablespoon
- teaspoon
- wire cooling rack
- oven gloves

To Make

1. Arrange the shelves and turn on the oven to heat. Prepare the sandwich tins (see page 7).
2. Pour 1 pint of water into the pan and place on a low heat.
3. Sieve the flour and baking powder on to the plate.
4. Break the eggs into the teacup and pour into the bowl.
5. Add the sugar.
6. Lay the bowl on top of the pan of warm water and whisk the eggs and sugar together. As you do this the mixture will become thick and creamy. The heat of the water begins to cook the eggs and this helps to trap more air into the mixture.
7. When the mixture is very thick and creamy, turn off the heat. Use oven gloves to lift the bowl off the pan on to a dish towel.
8. Add the flour and water and gently fold in (see page 8).
9. Put equal amounts of the mixture into each sandwich tin. Smooth the top and tap each tin on the worktop – this helps to even out the mixture.
10. Use the oven gloves to put the tins in the oven and bake for 20 minutes.

11 Remove the tins from the oven using oven gloves. Loosen the edges by running the palette knife all round the tin. Tap each tin on the worktop and turn out the sponges on to the cooling rack.

12 Wash your dirty utensils while the sponges are cooling.

13 Use the tweezers to remove the green leaves and core from the strawberries. Put them in the sieve and wash them under cold running water. Drain well. Put them in a small bowl.

14 Add the sugar to the strawberries and mash them with the fork.

15 Separate the egg white from the yolk (see page 10). Put the egg white in the small bowl and whisk until stiff.

16 Put the cream in the other small bowl and whisk until stiff (you must beat the egg white before the cream because any cream sticking to the whisk would prevent the egg white from whipping to a froth).

17 Put the cream and egg whites into the mixing bowl. Add the strawberries and fold everything together using the tablespoon.

18 Put one sponge on the plate (make sure the sponge is cold!). Spread the strawberry mixture over the top with the palette knife; place the other sponge on top of this. Shake some caster sugar over the whole sponge for a really professional finish!

19 Phew! Sit down and enjoy all your hard work. You can serve your Scottish Strawberry Sandwich as a dessert with pouring cream or for afternoon tea.

Small three-pronged forks are used to eat cakes which would otherwise be difficult to 'handle'. These forks have a thick prong at one side with two thinner prongs beside it and are called 'pastry forks'.

Selkirk Bannock

Inter

Needs left for 45 mins

2 hrs

Cook

Oven ☐ 1 hr 30 mins

Gas 4, 350°F or 180°C

middle shelf

This famous bannock, which is actually more like a cake, comes from the Border town of Selkirk. It is a rich, yeasted cake which is shaped like a cob loaf and is the Scottish equivalent of the English lardy cake. It was traditionally made with left-over dough from the weekly bread-making. Up until the eighteenth century Selkirk Bannocks were only made for festive occasions. There were two reasons for this: the first was that the ingredients were difficult to obtain and very, very expensive and, secondly, a law had been passed that prohibited bakers from making anything but plain breads, except for special occasions. You don't need to wait for a special occasion – you can make Selkirk Bannock now!

Have Ready

450g (1lb) flour
225g (8oz) sultanas
110g (4oz) sugar
50g (2oz) butter
50g (2oz) lard
50g (2oz) chopped mixed peel
150ml (1/4 pint) milk
6g (1/4oz) dried yeast

Glaze

1 tablespoon milk
1 tablespoon sugar

900g (2lb) loaf tin, lined and oiled *(see page 7)*
mixing bowl
2 saucepans
sieve
teacup
pastry brush
wooden spoon
tablespoon
teaspoon
tea towel or clingfilm
polythene bag
wire cooling rack
oven gloves

To Make

1. Sieve the flour and sugar into the bowl. Add the yeast and mix well.
2. Put the butter and lard into a saucepan and place on a low heat. Watch it carefully and remove from the heat as soon as the lard and butter have melted.
3. Pour the milk into the other saucepan and place on a low heat. Remove from the heat when the milk is just warm (blood heat) and pour into the melted fat.
4. Make a hole in the middle of the flour, sugar and yeast and pour in the melted fat and milk. Mix well to make a smooth dough.
5. Cover the bowl with a warm, damp tea towel or clingfilm and leave in a warm place for 45 minutes, or until the dough doubles in size (this is called 'proving').
6. Arrange the shelves and turn on the oven to heat.

7. Put some flour on your hands and knead the dough for about 5 minutes (see page 9). (This is called 'knocking down' and makes sure that the air is evenly distributed through the dough.)
8. Add the sultanas and mixed peel and knead well for a further 5 minutes to mix everything together.
9. Lift the dough into the loaf tin. Place the loaf tin inside the polythene bag and tie the top loosely. Put back in the warm place for 20 minutes to rise again.
10. Take the tin out of the polythene bag. Use the oven gloves to place the tin in the oven and bake for 1 hour.
11. Mix the milk and sugar in the teacup until the sugar has dissolved.
12. Take the tin out of the oven using the oven gloves and set on a heat-resistant surface. Use the pastry brush to brush the water and sugar over the top.
13. Place the tin back in the oven (remember to use the oven gloves!) and bake for 20 minutes. Test the cake with the skewer – if it comes out wet, bake the cake for a further 10 minutes.
14. Remove the tin from the oven using the oven gloves and set on the wire rack to cool in the tin. Knock the base of the tin with a spoon, the cake will sound hollow when ready.
15. Store in an airtight container. Eat cut into thick wedges – delicious!

Vinegar Cake

Adv

1 hr 20 mins

Cook

Oven □
1 hr

Gas 4, 350°F
or 180°C

middle shelf

Freeze

This is an economical recipe for a family cake – it is easy to make and contains no eggs. In fact, Vinegar Cake is a wartime recipe: during the war eggs were difficult to get.

Have Ready

- 225g (8oz) flour
- 175g (6oz) mixed fruit
- 110g (4oz) sugar
- 75g (3oz) margarine
- 3 tablespoons milk
- 2 tablespoons vinegar
- 1 level teaspoon bicarbonate of soda

- cake tin (18cm or 7″) lined and oiled *(see page 6)*
- mixing bowl
- sieve
- teacup
- measuring jug
- wooden spoon
- tablespoon
- teaspoon
- knife
- plate
- skewer
- wire cooling rack
- oven gloves

To Make

1. Arrange the shelves and turn on the oven to heat.
2. Sieve the flour into the bowl.
3. Cut the margarine into small pieces on the plate and rub into the flour using your fingers (see page 8).
4. Add the sugar and the dried fruit.
5. Measure the vinegar into the jug and add 2 tablespoons of milk.
6. Put 1 tablespoon of milk in the teacup and add the bicarbonate of soda. Stir well to dissolve it.
7. Hold the jug over the bowl and pour in the contents of the teacup. The mixture will froth up. Quickly pour this liquid into the bowl and mix it well.
8. Quickly pour the mixture into the prepared tin and use oven gloves to put it in the oven. Bake for 20 minutes then turn down the oven heat to Gas 3, 325°F or 170°C and bake for 40 minutes.
9. Remove the cake from the oven using oven gloves. Test with a skewer. Place the tin on the wire rack to cool.
10. When the Vinegar Cake is cold, take it out of the tin and store in an airtight container. It is delicious cut into thick wedges on its own or spread with butter.

Granny's Loaf

This recipe comes from the Highlands – the cake tastes just like a Clootie Dumpling. A Clootie or Cloutie dumpling is a traditional spicy fruit pudding or cake which is cooked by boiling it in a 'clout' or cloth.

Have Ready

225g (8oz) mixed sultanas and currants

2 eggs

2 teacups flour

1 cup water

1 cup soft brown sugar

75g (3oz) margarine

1 teaspoon cinnamon

1 teaspoon ground ginger

1 teaspoon bicarbonate of soda

1 teaspoon baking powder

900g (2lb) loaf tin, lined and oiled *(see page 7)*

large pan

skewer

2 teacups

wooden spoon

tablespoon

teaspoon

small bowl

fork

sieve

wire cooling rack

oven gloves

To Make

1. Put the water, sugar, margarine, fruit and spices into the pan.
2. Place the pan on a medium heat and bring to the boil. Turn off the heat and leave to cool for 30 minutes.
3. Arrange the shelves and turn on the oven to heat.
4. Break the eggs into a teacup, pour into the small bowl and beat with the fork.
5. Sieve the flour and bicarbonate of soda into the pan. Add the eggs and beat together with the wooden spoon.
6. Pour the mixture into the oiled and lined loaf tin.
7. Use the oven gloves to place the tin in the oven. Bake for 1 hour. Test with a skewer. If the skewer comes out damp, bake for a further 15 minutes.
8. Use the oven gloves to remove the tin from the oven and set on the wire rack to cool in the tin.
9. When your Granny's Loaf is cold, remove it from the tin and cut into thick slices. Try sprinkling it with caster sugar and heating it quickly under the grill – serve it with ice-cream for a really scrumptious pudding!

Inter

1 hr 45 mins

Cook

Oven ☐ 1 hr

Gas 4, 350°F or 180°C

middle shelf

Freeze ✳

Dundee Cake

Inter

2 hrs

Cook

Oven
1 hr 30 mins

Gas 3, 325°F
or 170°C

below middle

Freeze

In his book about Skipness on the Mull of Kintyre, Angus Graham describes the picnic lunches they were given 'on the hill' while out shooting. 'The lunches consisted of cold meat sandwiches made in the kitchens and a piece of cake . . . with a supply of whisky and some bottles of soda water.' He wrote this in the 1880s when Dundee Cake became a great favourite. Today the delicious cake, topped with whole, roasted almonds, is still one of the most famous Scottish tea table specialities.

If you do not like a dark cake, a Dundee Cake makes an ideal Christmas cake.

Have Ready

225g (8oz) flour
175g (6oz) butter
150g (5oz) caster sugar
4 eggs
1 level teaspoon baking powder
25g (1oz) blanched, split almonds
38g (1½oz) mixed peel
75g (3oz) currants
75g (3oz) raisins
75g (3oz) sultanas

Glaze

2 tablespoons milk
1 tablespoon sugar

17cm (7″) round cake tin, lined and oiled *(see page 6)*
saucepan
3 mixing bowls
small bowl
sieve
bowl scraper
wooden spoon
tablespoon
teaspoon
teacup
fork
pastry brush
wire cooling rack
oven gloves

To Make

1. Arrange the shelves and turn on the oven to heat.
2. Put the fruit in a mixing bowl.
3. Sieve the flour and baking powder into another bowl.
4. Put the butter and sugar in the third bowl and cream with the wooden spoon until light and creamy.
5. Break each egg into the cup and pour into the small bowl. Beat together with the fork.
6. Add a spoonful of flour and a quarter of the egg to the butter and sugar mixture. Beat well. Repeat until all the egg is used.
7. Carefully fold in the rest of the flour with the tablespoon (see page 8).
8. Add the fruit and stir in gently – reach right down into the bowl and make sure it is all mixed well together.
9. Scrape the mixture into the prepared tin, making sure that it is evenly spread around the tin and level the top with the bowl scraper. Wet your hands and use your palms to flatten the top of the cake – this will help stop the cake from rising in a peak in the middle.

10 Lay the almonds on top: work your way round the edge of the cake. Then lay another ring of almonds inside this one. Keep working in towards the middle of the cake until the top is covered.

11 Use the oven gloves to put the cake in the oven. Bake for 1 hour 30 minutes.

12 Boil the milk and sugar in the saucepan. Turn off the heat.

13 Take the cake from the oven (using the oven gloves) 10 minutes before it is ready and set on a heat-resistant surface.

14 Use the pastry brush to paint the milk and sugar over the top of the cake.

15 Put the cake back in the oven (remember the oven gloves!) to finish cooking.

16 Remove the cake from the oven using the oven gloves and test with a skewer. If it is wet in the middle, put the cake back in the oven and bake for a further 15 minutes and test again. (The secret of a good moist fruit cake is long slow cooking and plenty of patience!)

17 Remove from the oven with the oven gloves and set on the wire rack to cool in the tin. Store in an airtight container. It really will be worth all the effort once you have tasted this delicious cake.

Black Bun

Adv

5 hrs

Cook

Oven
4 hrs

Gas 3, 325°F
or 170°C

below middle

Black Bun is a rich fruit cake which is traditionally eaten at Hogmanay. In the original recipe a bread dough pastry case was filled with a rich fruit and spice mixture – the pastry was made using a piece of dough left over from the weekly bread making! The recipe varied from area to area, each housewife having her own particular recipe. Some used to keep the black bun for a whole year before it was eaten!

Have Ready

225g (8oz) currants
225g (8oz) raisins
175g (6oz) ready-made shortcrust pastry
110g (4oz) flour
50g (2oz) chopped almonds
50g (2oz) mixed peel
25g (1oz) sugar
1 egg
1 tablespoon brandy
1 level teaspoon ground cinnamon
1 level teaspoon ground ginger
1 level teaspoon allspice
1 level teaspoon bicarbonate of soda
pinch black pepper

900g (2lb) loaf tin, well oiled *(see page 7)*
mixing bowl
teacup
knife + fork
ruler
wooden spoon
teaspoon
rolling pin
bowl scraper
pastry brush
skewer
wire cooling rack
oven gloves

To Make

1. Arrange the shelves and turn on the oven to heat.
2. To calculate the size of pastry you will need: measure the length of the loaf tin. Measure the depth and multiply by two. Add this to the length. Measure the depth and width of the loaf tin and multiply by two. This is the length and width of your rolled pastry.
3. Shake some flour on the worktop and roll out the pastry a little larger than the measurements you have calculated.
4. Cut off a piece the size of the top of the tin. This will be the 'lid' of your Black Bun.
5. Lift the pastry up and over the rolling pin and use the rolling pin to lift the pastry. Lower the pastry into and over the tin and off the rolling pin. Gently press the pastry against the bottom and sides of the tin with your knuckles.
6. Break the egg into the cup and beat it with the fork.
7. Put the flour in the mixing bowl. Add the spices, bicarbonate of soda and sugar and mix well.
8. Add the dried fruit and almonds.
9. Add the brandy and most of the egg to the mixture and mix well together.

10 Pour the fruit mixture into the pastry case and flatten the top with the back of the bowl scraper.

11 Dip the pastry brush in water and use it to moisten the edges of the pastry.

12 Lay the lid on top and pinch round the edges with your thumb and forefinger to seal it.

13 Use the skewer to pierce four holes right through the lid to the bottom of the tin. Brush the top with the rest of the beaten egg.

14 Use the oven gloves to place the tin in the oven and bake for 4 hours – plenty of time for you to take a rest after all your hard work!

15 Check the Black Bun after 3 hours – if it looks too brown on top, lay a double sheet of greaseproof paper on the top. Reduce the oven temperature to Gas 2, 300°F or 150°C. Bake for a further hour.

16 Take the tin out of the oven using oven gloves and set on the wire rack. Leave to cool in the tin.

17 Now you'll have to wait some more as you should keep your Black Bun for several weeks in an airtight container before eating it! I hope you'll think it was worth the wait!

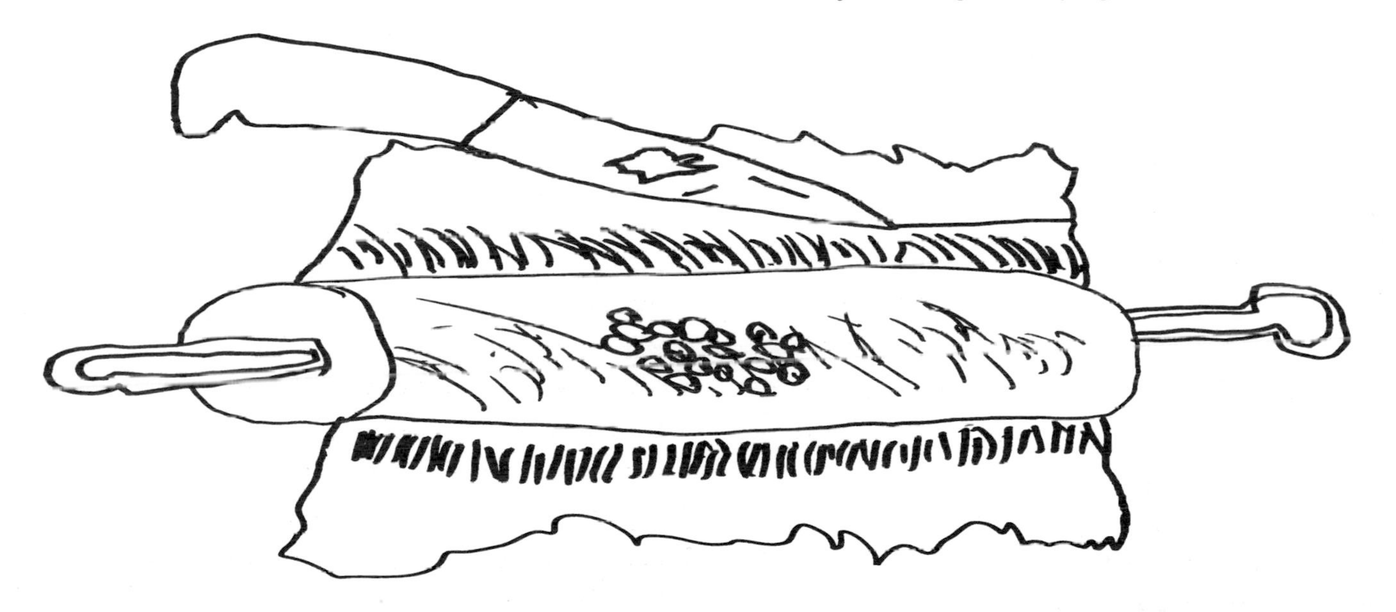

Berwickshire Fruit Loaf

The typical Scottish home was a two-roomed cottage called a 'but 'n' ben'. The 'but' was the kitchen and living-room where the family cooked, ate and lived.

Inter

2 hrs

Cook

Oven
1 hr

Gas 4, 350°F or 180°C

middle shelf

Freeze

Have Ready

- 450g (1lb) currants
- 350g (12oz) flour
- 110g (4oz) rice flour
- 110g (4oz) caster sugar
- 110g (4oz) margarine
- 330ml (½ pint) milk
- 25g (1oz) chopped peel
- 1 teaspoon bicarbonate of soda

- 900g (2lb) loaf tin, lined and oiled *(see page 7)*
- mixing bowl
- measuring jug
- wooden spoon
- tablespoon
- teaspoon
- skewer
- sieve
- plate
- knife
- wire cooling rack
- oven gloves

To Make

1. Arrange the shelves and turn on the oven to heat.
2. Sieve the flour and rice flour into the bowl.
3. Cut the margarine into small pieces on the plate. Add to the bowl and use your fingers to rub it into the flour (see page 8).
4. Add the currants, caster sugar and chopped peel and mix well with the wooden spoon.
5. Measure the milk into the jug and add the bicarbonate of soda. Pour into the bowl and mix to a soft consistency. If the mixture is too stiff, add a little more milk.
6. Pour the mixture into the lined and oiled loaf tin and use the oven gloves to put it into the oven. Bake for 1 hour.
7. Remove from the oven using the oven gloves and test the fruit loaf with a skewer – if it is still soft in the middle put it back in the oven to bake for another 10 minutes.
8. Remove the tin from the oven (remember to use oven gloves!) and set on the wire rack to cool in the tin.
9. When the loaf is cold, remove it from the tin and cut into thick slices. Serve your Berwickshire Fruit Loaf with butter or honey – it tastes good with cheese!

Drinks

A lot of Scottish words are really corruptions of French words. The French influence is a long one, dating back to the thirteenth century when Scotland and France joined forces against the English. As a result of this 'Auld Alliance' trade, fashion, food and language were shared between the two countries. The old Scottish words associated with drinking are mostly French in origin, for example: tassie (cup) from the French *tasse*; bauvrage (a drink or beverage) from *beuvrage*; verry (glass or tumbler) from *verre*; and acornie (a drinking vessel with handles) from *acorne*.

Scotland's first national drink was claret, a wine imported from France in the days of the Auld Alliance. Claret was taken round the streets in barrels from which it was sold by the jugful. Later, working men preferred to drink ale and Burns speaks of ale – not whisky – as the Scotch drink. It was not until the seventeenth century that whisky became so important. A law was passed by the Scottish Privy Council forbidding the import of wines. The heavy taxation on wine which followed made claret too expensive and so whisky became popular.

Tea was introduced in the late seventeenth century by Mary of Modena, the wife of James VII of Scotland and II of England.

There are many traditional home-made drinks which are simple and cheap to make and very good to drink.

Simple

3 hrs

No Cook ☒

Barley Water

'When the doctor disapproves of Lemon Juice,' Lady Clark of Tillypronie recommends Barley Water to anyone feeling ill. It always makes me feel better!

Have Ready

50g (2oz) pearl barley

25g (1oz) sugar

rind and juice of a lemon

570ml (1 pint) boiling water

1 litre (1¾ pint) heat-proof jug

plate large enough to cover the jug

lemon squeezer

grater

measuring jug

small sieve

wooden spoon

To Make

1. Wash and dry the lemon. Grate the rind on to the plate. Cut the lemon in half and squeeze out the juice (see page 10).
2. Put the rind, juice, sugar and barley into the jug and pour in the boiling water.
3. Put the plate over the jug and leave until cold.
4. When the Barley Water is cold, give it a stir with wooden spoon, then strain it through the sieve into the measuring jug.
5. Dilute your Barley Water to taste with cold water.
6. Keep covered in the fridge and use within 3 days. Barley Water is very refreshing and very good for you.

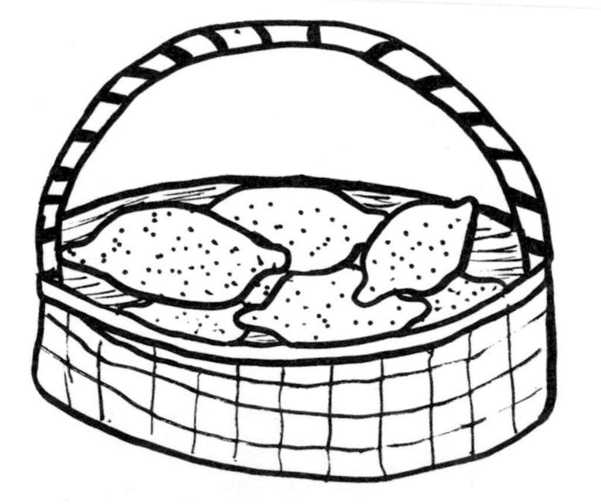

Old Fashioned Lemonade

*This drink can be made with oranges, grapefruit or a mixture of all three! I suppose if you used lemons, oranges **and** grapefruits you would call it a Three-fruit Squash!*

Simple

3 hrs

No Cook ☒

Have Ready

- 2 fresh lemons
- 110g (4oz) sugar
- 570ml (1 pint) boiling water
- 1 litre (1¾ pint) heat-proof jug
- wooden spoon
- grater
- lemon squeezer
- small sieve
- measuring jug
- plate to cover the jug
- knife

To Make

1. Wash and dry the lemon. Grate the rind on to a plate and scrape it into the jug. Wash and dry the plate.
2. Cut the lemons in half, squeeze out the juice (see page 10) and pour it into the jug.
3. Add the sugar to the jug and pour in 1 pint of boiling water.
4. Stir with the wooden spoon and cover with the plate.
5. Leave to cool.
6. When the lemonade is cold, strain it through the small sieve into the measuring jug. Leave to drain for 10 minutes and throw the rind away.
7. Dilute to taste with cold water.
8. Keep covered in the fridge and use within 3 days. Lemonade makes a good drink to soothe a sore throat – just mix it with some hot water and a little honey.

Raspberry Vinegar

Inter

Needs to infuse for 1 month between step 4 and step 5

Steps 1–4: 40 mins
Steps 5–8: 1hr 30 mins
Bottling: 2 hrs

Cook

Hob

This is a refreshing summer drink, made from newly picked raspberries. It takes a month before it is ready to drink, but it is worth waiting for!
The amount of Raspberry Vinegar you will get depends on how juicy the raspberries are.

Have Ready

900g (2lb) fresh raspberries

1 bottle white wine vinegar

1 kg (2.2lb) granulated sugar

900g (2lb) jar with a tight-fitting lid

stew pan

large bowl or jug

breakfast cup or mug (275ml or ½ pint)

sieve

ladle

2 screw-top bottles

wooden spoon

tablespoon

plate

jug

oven gloves

To Make

1 Fill the jar with the fresh raspberries and then pour in as much vinegar as you can. Place the jar in the pan.

2 Pour enough water into the pan to come halfway up the side of the jar. Put the pan on the heat. When the water begins to boil, turn down the heat until just bubbling and carefully place the jar in the water (cooking in this way is called a 'water bath').

3 Cook for 30 minutes. Turn off the heat and use oven gloves to lift the jar on to a heat-resistant surface. Leave to cool.

4 Put the lid on the jar. Leave in a cool, safe place for 1 month.

5 After 1 month, put the sieve over the bowl and pour in the contents of the jar. Leave to drain for 10 minutes.

6 Measure the juice into the pan using the cup or mug – for every mug or cup of juice add 225g (8oz) sugar.

7 Put the pan on a medium heat. Stir with the wooden spoon to dissolve the sugar and slowly bring to the boil. Turn down the heat so that it is just bubbling. Leave the wooden spoon in the pan – this will prevent the juice from boiling over.

8 Boil for 1 hour.

9 Turn off the heat and leave to cool. Use the tablespoon to carefully lift off any scum from the top of the juice.

10 Ladle the juice into the jug (hold it over the pan to avoid drips) and then pour it into the clean bottles.

11 Label the bottles with the name and date and keep them in a cool place.

12 Dilute to taste with cold water. Raspberry Vinegar is good diluted with sparkling water and lots of ice – a taste of summer long after it is past.

Stokos

This is a drink which was made at harvest time to refresh the men, women and children as they worked in the field gathering the grain.

Simple

Needs left for 2–3 hrs

10 mins

No Cook ☒

Have Ready

- 25g (1oz) oatmeal
- 38g (½oz) sugar
- juice of half a lemon
- 1 litre (¾ pint) boiling water

- large soup pot
- measuring jug
- wooden spoon
- measuring jug
- large bowl
- sieve
- clean, screw-top bottles
- ladle

To Make

1. Put the oatmeal and sugar into the pot, pour in the lemon juice and a little warm water and mix well. Put the pan on the hob.
2. Carefully pour in the boiling water, stirring all the time. Turn on the heat and bring the pan to the boil.
3. Boil for 3 minutes.
4. Turn off the heat and leave to cool in the pan.
5. Place the sieve over the bowl and strain the cold liquid into the bowl.
6. Use the ladle to pour the juice into the jug.
7. Pour into the bottles, label with the name and date. Keep in the fridge and use within 3 days. Dilute to taste with cold water.

Stoorum

This traditional drink is called 'Stoor-a-drink' in Shetland. In the Hebrides, folk made a similar drink using barley-meal instead of oatmeal. You can try making both and see which you prefer.

Simple

10 mins

Cook

Hob

Have Ready

- 1 heaped teaspoon oatmeal
- 4 teaspoons cold water
- 150ml (¼ pint) boiling water
- 150ml (¼ pint) boiling milk
- salt

- saucepan
- half-pint mug
- measuring jug
- teaspoon

To Make

1. Put the oatmeal and water into the mug and stir to a smooth paste with the teaspoon.
2. Measure the milk in the jug and pour into the saucepan. Place the pan on the heat to boil. Watch it all the time to make sure that the milk does not boil over. Turn off the heat.
3. Half fill the mug with boiling water. Stir well.
4. Pour the boiling milk into the mug. Stir well.
5. Add salt to taste and drink your Stoorum while it is hot.

Simple

10 mins

No Cook ☒

Quick Blackcurrant Drink

Blackcurrants are full of Vitamin C and are very good for you. A hot blackcurrant drink is very comforting on a cold day. All you need for this drink is some blackcurrant jam and hot water!

Have Ready

- 1 dessertspoonful blackcurrant jam
- 275ml (½ pint) boiling water
- honey or sugar
- lemon juice

- dessertspoon
- heat-proof jug
- measuring jug
- small sieve or strainer
- half-pint mug
- plate to cover the jug

To Make

1. Put the jam into the heat-proof jug and add the boiling water. Stir with the dessertspoon and cover with the plate.
2. Leave in a warm place for 5 minutes (the water will become flavoured by the jam – this is called 'infusing').
3. Strain through the small sieve into the mug.
4. Add honey or sugar and lemon juice to taste.
5. Drink immediately. This is a good bedtime drink when you have a cold or sore throat.

Jams, Marmalades and Preserves

Scottish housewives have always been proud of their home-made jams, marmalades and preserves. They were a favourite accompaniment to the home-made scones, bannocks and breads of the Scottish High Tea Table. Raspberry and strawberry jams are probably the best known but folk also made good use of the wild fruits which grew on the moors and in the hedgerows.

Elizabeth Grant of Rothiemurcus describes a visit to her aunt and uncle, Captain and Mrs Grant, who lived nearby at Inverdruie.

'They kept a cupboard next the fire – it was quite a pantry. Oatcakes, barley scones, flour scones, butter, honey, sweetmeats, cheese and wine and spiced whisky all came out of the deep shelves of this agreeable recess, as did the great key of the dairy.

'Old Mary, the cook, skimmed off the fine rich cream [from the milk], which Mrs Grant would afterwards pour on a whole pot of jam and give us it for lunch. This dish, under the name of "bainne briste", or broken milk, is a great favourite wherever it has been introduced.'

Important: Before You Begin

1) **Jam-making** – Making jam involves working with very hot liquids – you must be very careful. Always ask an adult for permission before you begin making the jam.

2) **Preparing the Fruit –** Put the fruit in a colander or large sieve and wash it under running water. Drain. Top and tail the fruit by cutting off the stalks and leaves with kitchen scissors. You do this with blackcurrants, rosehips and gooseberries. Cut off stalks from rowans, blaeberries and elderberries. Hulling is done by pulling out the leaf and core from strawberries, raspberries and loganberries with a pair of tweezers, sugar tongs or your thumb and forefinger. To take out the seeds or stones: cut the fruit in half, ease out the stone or seeds using either the tip of the knife or a teaspoon. We do this with rosehips, plums, cherries and geans.

3) **Sticking** – Rub a little butter round the inside of the pan to prevent the jam from sticking.

4) **Scum** – A frothy scum may form on the jam as it is cooking. This can be dispersed by stirring in a little piece of butter. Dip a large spoon in hot water and then carefully use it to skim off any scum from the top of the jam on to a plate.

5) **Boiling** – You must make sure all the sugar has dissolved before the jam boils. Once the sugar and fruit have come to the boil, keep it on a rapid boil. Leave the wooden spoon in the jam while it is boiling and this will help to stop it from boiling over.

6) **Using a Jelly Bag** – A jelly bag is used to drain the juice from the fruit pulp. You need to suspend the jelly bag over a bowl to catch the juice. Lay a a wooden pole (a brush handle is ideal) across two chairs or tables. Slip the handles of the jelly bag over the pole and place a bowl underneath. Make sure that the jelly bag is hanging directly over the top of the bowl. Pour the pulp into the bag and leave it to drain, overnight is best. Do not be tempted to force or squeeze the juices through the bag – if you do the jelly will be cloudy.

7) **Setting Test** – Put a little jam on a cold plate and leave it to cool. It should form a skin and wrinkle when you push it with your finger. If it does not, keep boiling the jam and test every 3 or 4 minutes.

8) **Pouring** – Jelly should be poured into jars as soon as it is ready. However, jam needs to cool a little and then stirred to mix the fruit before it is poured into jars. Keep a damp cloth handy to wipe any spills before they set.

9) **Covering** – Cover the jar of hot jam with a clean screw-top lid. As the jar cools it creates a vacuum which helps to keep the jam from going bad. Jam pot covers can be purchased from supermarkets. Carefully press the wax disc on to the surface of the jam and secure the plastic cover with a rubber band placed round the rim of the jar. Do this when the jam is cold. Label with the name and date and store in a cool place.

Blaeberry Jam

These small, blue berries can be found growing among the heather on the moors and also among the grasses along the cliff tops. They have a juicy and very distinctive flavour – you will have blue fingers when you have been out picking them and a blue tongue after tasting them!

Adv

1 hr

Cook

Hob

Have Ready

1kg 350g (3lb) blaeberries

225g (8oz) thin red rhubarb

1kg 350g (3lb) granulated sugar

12.5g (½oz) butter

preserving pan

wooden spoon

colander

saucer

kitchen scissors

8 jam jars with lids or covers

sharp knife

chopping board

ladle

baking tray

heat-proof jug

oven gloves

To Make

1. Read the opposite page thoroughly before you start.
2. Remove any stems or leaves from the blaeberries. Wash the blaeberries and drain well.
3. Wash the rhubarb well under cold running water. Cut into pieces about 2cm (1 inch) long on the chopping board and put them in the pan.
4. Add the sugar and put the pan on a medium heat. Stir the rhubarb and sugar until the sugar has all dissolved and the mixture is boiling.
5. Turn down the heat until the mixture is just bubbling and boil for 10 minutes. Stir occasionally.
6. Add the blaeberries and mix well. Turn up the heat until the jam boils, then boil rapidly for 20 minutes. Stir in the butter.
7. Test the jam on the saucer (see page 100). When it has set, turn off the heat. Put the jars and the jug on the baking tray beside the pan. Leave the jam to cool for 5 minutes.
8. Stir the jam and ladle it into the jug. Carefully pour the jam into the jars. Cover the hot jars with screw-top lids or leave them to cool and put on the jam pot covers.
9. Label with the date and name. Blaeberry Jam has a taste all its own and is particularly good on top of cream cheese spread on freshly baked scones!

Rosehip Jelly

In the autumn rosehips can be seen in all the hedgerows and woods around the countryside. An afternoon's walk can provide you with enough berries to make this lovely jelly. Make sure you pick only the reddest of berries to ensure that the jelly will be a beautiful rose-red colour. The fruit must be cooked in an enamel pan so that it keeps its lovely colour.

Adv

Needs to drain overnight

4 hrs

Cook

Hob

Have Ready

275ml (½ pint) rosehips

1kg 350g (3lb) crab apples

sugar

12.5g (½oz) butter

preserving pan

large enamel pan

large bowl

colander

sharp knife

chopping board

teaspoon

saucer

ladle

8 jam jars with lids or covers

baking tray

jelly bag

measuring jug

heat-proof jug

oven gloves

To Make

1 Read page 100 thoroughly before you start.

2 Wash the rosehips. Drain well. Cut them open on the chopping board and remove the seeds using the teaspoon. Throw away the seeds. Put the rosehips into the enamel pan.

3 Wash the crab apples. Drain them and cut them into quarters on the chopping board. Place in the enamel pan.

4 Put the pan on a low heat and cook the fruit very slowly and gently. This is called 'stewing' and it will remove all the juices from the rosehips. Stew for 2 hours. Turn off the heat.

5 Hang the jelly bag over the large bowl. Carefully ladle the fruit into the suspended jelly bag and leave to drain for as long as you can – overnight is best.

6 Rub a little butter round the inside of the preserving pan. Measure the juice into the pan using the jug. Add 450g (1lb) sugar for each 570ml (1 pint) of juice.

7 Put the pan on a medium heat. Stir until the sugar is dissolved and the jelly is boiling. Boil for 10 minutes.

8 Stir in 12.5g (½oz) of butter to disperse any scum.

9 Test the jam on the saucer (see page 100). When it has set, turn off the heat. Put the jars and the jug on the baking tray beside the pan. Leave the jelly to cool for 2 minutes.

10 Ladle the jelly into the jug. Carefully pour the jelly into the jars.

11 Cover the hot jars with screw top lids or leave them to cool before covering with jam pot covers.

12 Label with the date and name. Rosehip Jelly makes an unusual accompaniment to roast ham, roast turkey or chicken. It is also very good on home-made pancakes.

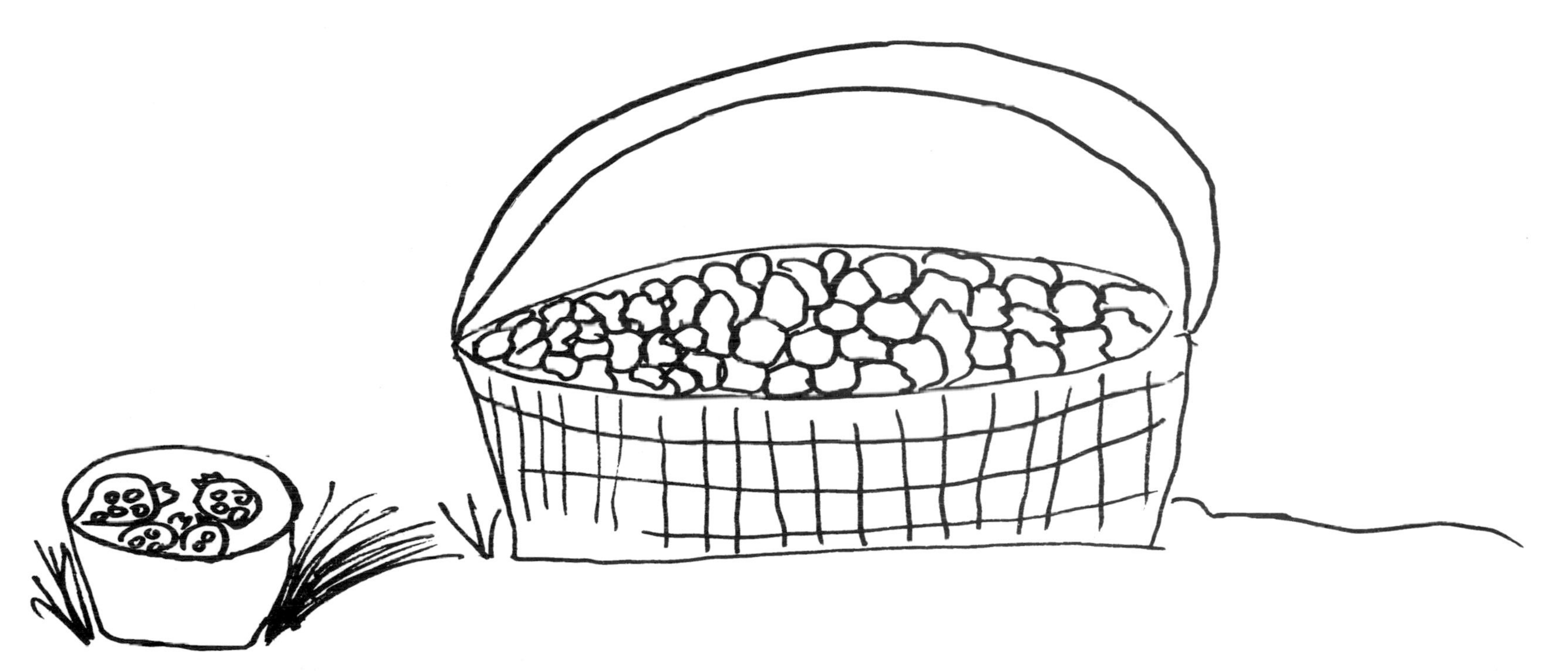

Rowan Jelly

Adv

Needs left overnight

1 hr

Cook

Hob

The Scots name for rowan is 'rodden'. There is a superstition that if a rowan tree (Mountain Ash) grows beside your house or church, it will protect you from evil. It was said to be unlucky to cut down a rowan tree. Pick bright red, ripe rowans for your jelly and serve as a traditional accompaniment to grouse, venison and other roast game. Rowan Jelly is also delicious on warm, newly baked barley bannocks.

Have Ready

- 1kg 350g (3lb) rowan berries
- sugar
- 4 apples
- water
- 12.5g (½oz) butter

- preserving pan
- large bowl
- jelly bag
- heat-proof jug
- measuring jug
- saucer
- ladle
- wooden spoon
- tablespoon
- 8 jam jars with lids or covers
- saucer
- baking tray
- colander
- kitchen scissors
- oven gloves

To Make

1. Read page 100 thoroughly before you start.
2. Cut the stalks off the rowans and wash them. Drain and put in the pan. Cover with water so that the berries float.
3. Put the pan on a medium heat. Bring to the boil and turn down the heat until the berries are simmering. Cook for 40 minutes until the water is red and the berries are soft.
4. Hang the jelly bag over the large bowl, pour the pulp into the jelly bag and leave overnight to drain.
5. Ladle the juice into the measuring jug and measure into the pan. Add 450g (1lb) of sugar for every 570ml (1 pint) of juice.
6. Put the pan on a medium heat and stir until all the sugar has dissolved. Bring the jelly to the boil. Boil for 30 minutes. Stir in the butter to disperse any scum.
7. Test the jam on the saucer (see page 100). When it has set, turn off the heat. Leave the jelly to cool for 5 minutes.
8. Put the jars and the heat-proof jug on the baking tray beside the pan. Ladle the jelly into the jug.
9. Carefully pour the jelly into the jars. Cover the hot jars with screw-top lids or leave to cool and put on the jam pot covers. Label with the date and name when cold.

Matrimony Jam

This jam will tell your fortune! Collect the damson stones from the jam you have on your plate and count them – the story is that they will tell who you will marry. Repeat this rhyme as you count each stone: 'Tinker, tailor, soldier, sailor, richman, poorman, beggarman or thief?' The answer depends on the number of stones you have!

Adv

1 hr 30 mins

Cook

Hob

Have Ready

- 450g (1 lb) damsons
- 450g (1 lb) apples (any variety)
- 450g (1 lb) pears (any variety)
- 570ml (1 pint) water
- 1.5kg (3½lb) sugar
- 12.5g (½oz) butter

- preserving pan
- baking tray
- heat-proof jug
- saucer
- ladle
- 8 jam jars with lids or covers
- wooden spoon
- tablespoon
- sharp knife
- chopping board
- potato peeler
- oven gloves

To Make

1. Read page 100 thoroughly before you start.
2. Rub a little butter round the inside of the pan.
3. Wash and drain the damsons, and put them in the pan. Pour in the water.
4. Peel the apples and pears with the potato peeler. Cut them into quarters on the chopping board and remove the cores and seeds. Throw the cores and seeds away.
5. Cut up the fresh roughly and add to the pan. Place on a medium heat and bring to the boil, stirring occasionally. Simmer for 20 minutes until the damsons are soft.
6. Reduce the heat and add the sugar. Stir until it has dissolved. Turn up the heat and bring the jam to the boil. Boil for 20 to 30 minutes. After 20 minutes, stir in 12.5g (½oz) of butter and test the jam (see page 100). When it has set, turn off the heat and leave to cool for 5 minutes.
7. Put the jars and jug on the tray beside the pan. Stir the jam well and ladle it into the jug. Pour the jam into the jars.
8. Cover the hot jars with screw-top lids or leave them to cool and put on the jam pot covers. Label with the date and name. Rememer to save the stones when you eat the jam to see who you will marry!

Adv

Needs to soak for 2 days

1 hr

Cook

Hob ◎

Oven □

Bramble and Rosehip Jam

You can make this jam just for the price of a walk in the countryside! Brambles and rosehips will be ripe at the same time in the autumn – October is a good month to go out in search of these fruits.

Have Ready

275ml (½ pint) rosehips

1kg 350g (3lb) brambles

sugar

12.5g (½oz) butter

preserving pan

large roasting tin

bowl

colander

saucer

ladle

wooden spoon

teaspoon

heat-proof jug

sharp knife

chopping board

measuring jug

8 jam jars with lids or covers

oven gloves

To Make

Wash and drain the rosehips. Cut them in half on the chopping board and scoop out the seeds with the teaspoon. Throw away the seeds. Chop the flesh into pieces and put in the bowl. Cover with cold water and leave to soak for 2 days.

1 Read page 100 thoroughly before you start.

2 After 1 day, put the brambles into the colander and wash under cold running water. Drain the brambles and put them in the roasting tin. Turn on the oven at its lowest setting and use the oven gloves to put the tray in the oven. Leave for about 6 hours and the heat will extract all the juices.

3 Remove the tray of brambles using the oven gloves and leave overnight.

4 Ladle the brambles and juice into the measuring jug and measure into the pan. Add 450g (1lb) of sugar for every 570ml (1 pint) of juice and fruit.

5 Place the colander in the sink and drain the water from the rosehips. Add them to the pan.

6 Put the pan on a medium heat. Stir until the sugar dissolves and the jam boils. Boil for 10 minutes.

7 Stir in the butter to disperse any scum on the jam.

8 Test the jam on the saucer (see page 100). When it has set, turn off the heat. Put the jars and the jug on the baking tray beside the pan. Leave the jam to cool for 5 minutes.

9 Stir the jam and ladle it into the jug. Carefully pour the jam into the jars.

10 Cover the hot jars with screw-top lids or leave them to cool and put on the jam pot covers.

11 Label with the date and name. Bramble and Rosehip Jam makes a lovely filling for sponge puddings – try it with the recipe for Dunfillin Blackberry Pudding in *Teach the Bairns to Cook* (page 102).

Adv

1 hr 15 mins

Cook

Hob

Raspberry Jam

Garden raspberries or wild raspberries can be used for this recipe. Wild raspberries can be found in woodlands or along the roadside growing in patches similar to brambles.

Have Ready

1kg 350g (3lb) raspberries

1kg 350g (3lb) sugar

12.5g (½oz) butter

preserving pan

baking tray

saucer

saucer

heat-proof jug

colander

ladle

wooden spoon

tablespoon

8 jam jars with lids or covers

oven gloves

To Make

1 Read page 100 thoroughly before you start.
2 Wash the fruit. Drain and put in the pan.
3 Put the pan on a medium heat and slowly bring to the boil. Boil steadily for 5 minutes.
4 Add the sugar and stir with the wooden spoon until the sugar has dissolved. Bring the jam to the boil and boil steadily for 5 minutes.
5 Stir in the butter to disperse any scum.
6 Test the jam on the saucer (see page 100) until it has set. Turn off the heat. Leave to cool for 5 minutes.
7 Put the jars and the jug on the baking tray beside the pan. Stir the jam well and ladle it into the jug. Carefully pour the jam into the jars.
8 Cover the hot jars with screw-top lids or leave them to cool and put on the jam pot covers.
9 Label with the date and name when cold. Home-made Raspberry Jam fills your house with a lovely smell as it cooks, and it makes an even better taste in your mouth when you eat it!

Wild Strawberry Jam

In Scotland, wild strawberries are called 'avern'. You can find them growing in the woodlands and along riverbanks. In his book describing life on the highland estate of Skipness at the end of the nineteenth century, Angus Graham remembers a typical afternoon tea:

'Tea was a sit-down meal with toast, scones, jam, honey, cake and so on. It took place at five o'clock, either in the school room or the hall, according to the size of the party. A really large party, perhaps with callers from outside, might demand two teapots.'

Adv

1 hr 30 mins

Cook

Hob

Oven

Have Ready

- 1kg 350g (3lb) wild strawberries
- 1kg 350g (3lb) sugar
- 12.5g (½oz) butter

- preserving pan
- large roasting tin
- baking tray
- wooden spoon
- heat-proof jug
- pair tweezers
- colander
- saucer
- 6 jam jars with lids or covers
- oven gloves

To Make

1. Read page 100 thoroughly before you start.
2. Turn on the oven to heat at Gas 1, 275°F or 140°C.
3. Hull, wash and drain the strawberries. Put them in the pan.
4. Put the pan on a medium heat and stir until the fruit boils. Turn down the heat and simmer gently for 20 minutes.
5. Put the sugar in the roasting tin and place it in the oven using oven gloves. Heat the sugar while the fruit is cooking.
6. Remove the tin from the oven using oven gloves (turn the oven off) and add the sugar to the fruit. Stir until the sugar is dissolved. Turn up the heat and boil for 15 minutes.
7. Test the jam on the saucer (see page 100) until it has set. Turn off the heat. Stir in the butter to disperse any scum and leave the jam to cool for 5 minutes.
8. Put the jars and jug on the baking tray beside the pan. Stir the jam well and then carefully ladle it into the jug.
9. Carefully pour the jam into the jars. Cover the hot jars with screw-top lids or leave them to cool and put on the jam pot covers. Label with the date and name.

Marmalade Jelly

Adv

Needs left overnight

2 hrs

Cook

Hob

During his tour of the Hebrides in 1773, Samuel Johnson wrote of the delicious breakfasts he was given:

'The breakfast, a meal which the Scots, whether of the Lowlands or mountains, must be confessed to excel us. The tea and coffee are accompanied not only with butter, but with honey, conserves and marmalades. If an epicure could remove by a wish, in quest of several gratifications, wherever he had supped he would breakfast in Scotland.'

Have Ready

- 1.8kg (4lb) bitter oranges
- 1.8kg (4lb) sugar
- 1.4 litres (2½ pints) water
- 2 lemons
- 12.5g (½oz) butter

- preserving pan
- baking tray
- large bowl
- small bowl
- ladle
- draining spoon
- wooden spoon
- dessertspoon
- large plate
- clingfilm
- sharp knife
- chopping board
- heat-proof jug
- jelly bag
- 10 jam jars with lids or covers
- oven gloves

To Make

1. Read page 100 thoroughly before you start.
2. Wash the fruit, put it in the pan, cover with water and put on a medium heat.
3. Bring to the boil and boil the fruit until it is tender (test with a skewer). This will take about 30 minutes. Turn off the heat.
4. Using the draining spoon, lift the fruit from the water on to the large plate. Leave to cool. Throw out the water.
5. Cut the cold fruit in half, scrape out the flesh into the pan (use the dessertspoon) and save the skin. Pour the measured water into the pan and put on a medium heat. Bring to the boil and boil for 30 minutes. Turn off the heat.
6. Cut the orange skins into fine shreds (strips) and put into the small bowl. Cover with clingfilm and leave in a cool place.
7. Suspend the jelly bag over the large bowl and pour the contents of the pan into the bag. Leave overnight to drain.
8. The following day, rub a little butter round the inside of the pan.

9 Throw away the pulp left in the jelly bag and pour the juice into the pan. Add the sugar and shredded skin and put the pan on a medium heat.

10 Stir until all the sugar has dissolved, then bring the pan to the boil and boil for 15 minutes.

11 Stir in 12.5g (½oz) of butter to disperse any scum on the top of the jelly.

12 Test the jelly (see page 100) on the plate until it has set. Turn off the heat and leave the jelly to cool for 5 minutes.

13 Put the jars and jug on the tray beside the cooker. Stir the jelly, ladle it into the jug and carefully pour it into the jars.

14 Cover and label when cold.

The Story of Marmalade

Marmalade is one of Scotland's most important contributions to the breakfast tables of the world. There are several stories as to how marmalade got its name – I will leave you to choose which one you think is best!

One story is that the first marmalade ever made was invented by one of Mary Queen of Scots' French chefs when she was ill. To coax her to eat, he made a jam of oranges, lemons and grapefruit and called it *Marie-Malade*. Translated from French, this means 'Mary is ill'. Through time, the phrase changed to marmalade.

During the reign of Mary Queen of Scots, merchant ships carrying oranges, lemons and grapefruit from Spain began arriving at Scottish ports. However, the fruit did not keep well and so it was made into a type of jam to preserve it. The Spanish word for jam is *marmelada* – perhaps this is how the word 'marmalade' came into our language.

Another story tells of how James Keiller, a poor Dundee grocer, bought some cheap, bitter seville oranges. His wife, who made quince jam, substituted oranges for the quinces and made orange jam instead. She put the jars of orange jam into the shop for sale and it became so popular that oranges were specially imported to make the jam. By 1797, several generations later, a factory was built in Dundee to produce the now world-famous Dundee marmalade. The Portuguese and Spanish word for a quince is *marmelo* and the word for jam is *marmelada* – do you think this is the real story behind marmalade?

Orange Jelly

Adv

Needs left overnight

1 hr

Cook

Hob

From the original marmalade recipe made hundreds of years ago there are now many different kinds of marmalade made to suit all tastes. This recipe is for those who do not like peel in their marmalade.

Have Ready

- 12 bitter seville oranges
- 3 sweet oranges
- 3 lemons
- sugar
- water
- 12.5g (½oz) butter

- preserving pan
- baking tray
- large bowl
- jelly bag
- ladle
- wooden spoon
- saucer
- heat-proof jug
- 2 teacups
- sharp knife
- chopping board
- 10 jam jars with lids or covers
- oven gloves

To Make

1. Read page 100 thoroughly before you start.
2. Wash the fruit and peel off the skins. Chop the skins roughly and add to the pan.
3. Cut the flesh into quarters and put in the pan. Add a cup of water for each orange.
4. Put the pan on a medium heat. Bring to the boil and reduce the heat. Simmer the fruit for 1 hour. Turn off the heat.
5. Suspend the jelly bag over the bowl and pour the contents of the pan into the jelly bag. Leave to drain overnight – do not be tempted to press the juice through the bag as this will cloud the jelly.
6. Rub round the inside of the pan with a little butter.
7. Throw away the pulp in the bag and use the teacup to measure the juice into the pan. Count the number of teacups of juice and then add the same number of sugar to the pan.
8. Put the pan on a medium heat. Stir until the sugar has dissolved and bring to the boil. Boil for 10 to 15 minutes. Stir in 12.5g (½oz) of butter to disperse any scum. Test the jelly (see page 100) until it has set. Turn off the heat.
9. Put the jars and jug on the baking tray beside the pan. Ladle the jelly into the jug and then pour into the jars, cover and label when cold.

Poor Man's Marmalade

In his book *Tours in Scotland*, written in 1760, Bishop Pococke describes eating toasted bread and a 'jelly of currants and preserved orange peel' at breakfast.
This old recipe wastes nothing.

Have Ready

450g (1lb) marmalade oranges

1 sweet orange

2 lemons

2.8 litres (5 pints) water

3kg (7lb) sugar

12.5g (½oz) butter

preserving pan

electric mincer, food processor or hand mincer

baking tray

ladle

wooden spoon

heat-proof jug

large bowl

plate or clingfilm

saucer

sharp knife

chopping board

10 jam jars with lids or covers

oven gloves

To Make

1. Read page 100 thoroughly before you start.
2. Wash the fruit, chop roughly and throw away the stones. Mince the fruit or put it through the food processor. If you do not have either, you can use the sharp knife to chop the fruit into very small pieces on the chopping board. Put the fruit into the large bowl
3. Pour in the water, cover with clingfilm or a large plate and leave to soak for 48 hours.
4. After 2 days, pour the water and fruit into the pan and put on a medium heat. Bring to the boil and boil for 30 minutes.
5. Add the sugar and stir until it is dissolved.
6. Bring back to the boil and boil for 45 minutes. Stir in the butter to disperse any scum on the top.
7. Test on the saucer (see page 100) until it has set. Turn off the heat and leave the marmalade to cool for 5 minutes.
8. Put the jars and jug on a tray beside the pan. Stir the marmalade well, ladle it into the jug and carefully pour it into the jars.
9. Cover and label when cold. Try marmalade on freshly baked scones, it is delicious!

Adv

Needs to soak for 2 days

2 hrs

Cook

Hob

Breakfast Orange Marmalade

This is a thick, tangy marmalade. In her book, *The Scots Kitchen*, F. Marian McNeill says 'Marmalade may be served with roast pork, duck or goose and with hot, boiled ham. Eaten with buttered oatcake, brown bread or wheaten meal scone, it is an excellent last mouthful at breakfast.'

Adv

Needs left overnight

1 hr

Cook

Hob

Have Ready

- 900g (2lb) seville bitter oranges
- 2 lemons
- 3.4 litres (6 pints) water
- 12.5g (½oz) butter
- sugar

- preserving pan
- baking tray
- large bowl
- small bowl
- ladle
- wooden spoon
- dessertspoon
- sharp knife
- chopping board
- measuring jug
- heat-proof jug
- small sieve
- saucer
- juice squeezer
- skewer
- 10 jam jars with lids or covers
- oven gloves

To Make

1. Read page 100 thoroughly before you start.
2. Wash the oranges and lemons. Cut them in half on the chopping board. Remove the stones and put them in the small bowl. Squeeze out the juice (see page 10) into the large bowl.
3. Cut the orange and lemon peel and pith into small strips and add to the bowl.
4. Cover the stones with some of the water and pour the rest into the bowl of fruit. Leave to soak overnight in a cool place.
5. Strain the water from the pips through the small sieve into the measuring jug – make a note of the amount of juice – and pour it into the pan.
6. Measure the pulp into the preserving pan – again, make a note of the amount.
7. Put the pan on a medium heat. Bring to the boil, turn down the heat and simmer for 30 minutes until the skins of the fruit are tender. (This can vary depending on the fruit). If you think that the skins are not soft enough, boil for a further 10 minutes. Test the skins with a skewer.

8 Add 450g (1lb) sugar for each 570ml (1 pint) of soaked fruit and water.

9 Stir until the sugar has dissolved. Turn up the heat and bring the marmalade to the boil. Boil for 30 minutes, stir in the butter and begin to test for setting (see page 100). The time it takes for the marmalade to reach setting point depends on the fruit you are using. When a set is achieved, turn off the heat.

10 Leave to cool for 5 minutes. The marmalade has to cool so that the peel is distributed throughout. If it is too hot, the peel will float; too cold and the thick jelly will trap air bubbles.

11 Put the jars and heat-proof jug on the tray beside the pan. Stir the marmalade well, ladle it into the jug and carefully pour it into the jars.

12 Cover the hot jars with screw-top lids or leave them to cool and put on the jam pot covers.

13 Label with the date and name when cold. If you like peel and the tangy taste of oranges, this marmalade is for you!

You can make Three-fruit Marmalade by using 2 grapefruits, 2 lemons and 2 sweet oranges instead of the oranges and lemons.

Adv

1 hr

Cook

Hob

Lemon Cheese or Curd

This is great old tea-time favourite – it can be spread on scones, pancakes or bread. It also makes a lovely filling for sponge cakes and biscuits.

Have Ready

225g (8oz) sugar
50g (2oz) butter
2 eggs
1 egg yolk
grated rind of a lemon
juice of 1½ lemons

stew pan
bowl which will sit on top of the pan
baking tray
plate
grater
teacup
lemon squeezer
small bowl
ladle
wooden spoon
fork
tea towel
heat-proof jug
6 jam jars with lids or covers
oven gloves

To Make

1. Grate the rind of the lemon and squeeze out the juice (see page 10).
2. Break each egg into the cup and pour into the small bowl.
3. Separate the egg yolk (see page 10) and it add to the whole eggs. Beat with the fork.
4. Quarter fill the pan with water and put on a medium heat. Heat the water until it is almost boiling.
5. Put the butter, sugar, eggs, lemon rind and juice into the bowl and sit it on top of the pan of hot water.
6. Stir with the wooden spoon until the sugar is dissolved and the mixture thickens. Do not let it to boil (the eggs will curdle like scrambled eggs). When it is ready it will coat the back of the spoon like thick honey. Turn off the heat.
7. Carefully, using oven gloves, lift the bowl on to a clean tea towel. Put the jars and jug on the baking tray beside the bowl.
8. Ladle the lemon curd into the jug and pour into the jars. Cover the hot jars with screw-top lids or leave them to cool and put on the jam pot covers. Label with the date and name when cool.
9. Keep in a cool place and refrigerate after opening.

Sweets

This book would not be complete without mention of our famous Scottish sweeties. There is a huge variety of sweets of different shapes and tastes – all made from very simple ingredients. Most of the recipes are not suitable for young children to make but perhaps your parents or grandparents will help you make these wonderful old fashioned sweets.

A long time ago, sweeties were only made at home – there were no shops with ready-made packets of sweets for sale. As time passed, those folk who were good at making sweets began to make extra and sell them in the streets, at market and at fairs. These women were known as 'sweetie wives'. This expression has survived – today, if someone is described as an 'old sweetie wife' it means they are a gossip! The original sweetie wives probably did talk a lot and spread the news as they sold their wares from place to place.

Home-made sweets such as marzipan dates and peppermint creams look good in small, brightly coloured paper cases. Save a nicely shaped box and cover it with wrapping paper, line the inside with coloured tissue paper and then lay a variety of sweets in their cases on top, close the lid and put a pretty tartan bow on top to make a really special present.

Important: Before You Begin

1) Use a large, strong, deep pan which will allow the contents to boil up – but stops them from spilling over on to the cooker!
2) Always make sure that the sugar has dissolved in the water or milk **before** it boils.
3) Brushing round the side of the pan with a pastry brush dipped in warm water will help to remove any sugar crystals which form as the mixture boils up.
4) **To test the mixture**: have ready a cup or small bowl filled with cold water. Drop a little of the sweetie mixture off the wooden spoon into the cold water and leave for a few minutes. Press the drop of toffee mixture with the back of a teaspoon and you can judge if the sweet is ready:

   (a) **Soft Ball**: the toffee feels soft and sticky.

   (b) **Hard Ball**: the toffee feels hard and does not stick to the spoon.

   (c) **Soft Crack Test**: as the toffee drops into the water it forms a strand. Lift it out of the water, it will snap easily.

   (d) **Hard Crack Test**: as above, but this time the strands of toffee are harder and will snap sharply.

The longer the sweetie mixture is boiled, the harder it will become. You must take great care not to boil the sweetie mixture for too long or it will become dark and bitter.

Glasgow Toffee or Cheugh Jeans

A Glasgow sweet-maker called Ball Allan was known as 'the Candy King'. He made a very tough, chewy toffee which he called Cheugh Jeans ('cheugh' means tough and very chewy). It was available in many different flavours – clove, peppermint, ginger, chocolate, vanilla and cinnamon. This is a recipe for chocolate-and-vanilla flavoured Cheugh Jeans.

Adv

55 mins

Cook

Hob

Have Ready

- 110g (4oz) golden syrup
- 75g (3oz) butter
- 75g (3oz) white sugar
- 75g (3oz) soft brown sugar
- 150ml (5 fl.oz) milk
- 25g (1oz) chocolate
- ½ teaspoon vanilla essence
- cooking oil

- strong soup pot
- baking tray, oiled *(see page 7)*
- wooden spoon
- teaspoon
- teacup
- sharp knife

To Make

1. Put the butter in the pan and heat gently until it is melted.
2. Add the butter, brown and white sugar, milk, syrup and chocolate. Keep stirring until the mixture boils.
3. Turn down the heat until the toffee is just boiling – if it boils too hard, it will spill over the side of the pan. Leave the wooden spoon in the pan to help stop the toffee from boiling over. Keep watching it.
4. After 15 minutes begin to test the toffee. Test it every 5 minutes until it forms a 'hard ball' (see page 118).
5. Remove the pan from the heat and set on a heat-resistant surface. Leave to cool for 5 minutes. Meanwhile, rub plenty of oil over the tray and the knife to stop the toffee from sticking.
6. Add the vanilla essence and stir well.
7. Carefully pour the toffee into the tin and leave to set. When it is still warm and almost set, cut into squares with the knife.
8. Store the cold toffee in an airtight tin to prevent it becoming sticky. You probably will not need the tin once you have tasted Cheugh Jeans!

Stories of Some Famous Scottish Sweeties

Edinburgh Rock was discovered by accident by a man called Alexander Fergusson during the late eighteenth century. His nick-name was 'Sweetie Sandy' for he made and sold sweets. One day he found some which had been forgotten; when he tasted them he found that they had become soft and crumbly in texture and had developed a light, delicate flavour. He began to make lots of these sweeties and called them Edinburgh Rock. Fergussons still make and sell Edinburgh Rock today.

The first **Jeddart Snails** (Jedburgh Snails) were made at the time of the Napoleonic Wars by a French prisoner of war for a Jedburgh baker. The recipe is still a secret. The sweets are dark-brown, peppermint-flavoured toffees.

Soor Plooms taste like sour plums! They are hard, round green balls with a very acid sour taste. The recipe comes from the Borders where a band of raiders from England were caught eating un-ripe (sour) plums.

Berwick Cockles are hard, peppermint flavoured sweets. They are shaped like cockle shells and are striped pink and white. Originally, they were made in Berwick and their shape represented the cockle shells found at the mouth of the River Tweed.

In 1833 a stone mason from Kirriemuir became blind. No longer able to continue in his job, he began to make and sell **Star Rock** candy. The secret recipe is still made and sold today in a small shop in the Roods in Kirriemuir.

Coltart's (pronounced Cooter) **Candy** was made in the Borders town of Melrose by a man called Coltart. He travelled around the area and was loved by the children who followed him as if he were the Pied Piper himself. He wrote the famous song 'Coltart's Candy', also known as 'Allie Ballie Bee', which tells of a young child sitting on his mother's knee 'greetin for a wee baw bee, tae buy some Coltart's Candy'. The sweets have an aniseed flavour, but the recipe was lost when Coltart died in 1890.

Moffat Toffees are not (as you would imagine from the name) soft and chewy sweets but hard, round amber balls with a gold stripe and tangy flavour. They are made in the Borders town of Moffat from a very old secret family recipe. In fact, there is a wonderful sweet shop in Moffat which sells Moffat Toffee along with a huge variety of other sweets – a sweetie lover's heaven!

Helensburgh Tablet

This toffee is really a type of Tablet or Taiblet and has a rich creamy flavour and a fudge-like texture.

Adv

I hr

Cook

Hob

Have Ready

900g (2lb) granulated sugar

110g (4oz) butter

150ml (1 gill) water

210g (7½ fl.oz) tin condensed milk

1 teaspoon vanilla essence

strong soup pot

baking tray, well oiled *(see page 7)*

wooden spoon

teaspoon

sharp knife

plastic bowl scraper

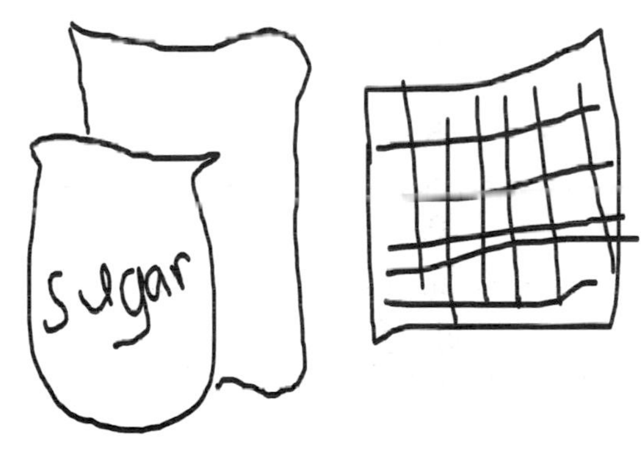

To Make

1 Put the sugar, butter, condensed milk and water (use the water to rinse out the milk tin) into the pan. Place on a medium heat and stir until the ingredients have dissolved. Bring the toffee to the boil.

2 Turn down the heat until the toffee is just bubbling in the pan. Simmer for 30 minutes, stirring frequently to prevent the toffee from sticking and burning. Leave the wooden spoon in the pan to help stop the toffee from boiling over.

3 Begin to test the toffee: test every 5 minutes. It is ready when it forms a soft ball in the bottom of the cup (see page 118).

4 Turn off the heat and set the pan on a heat-resistant surface. Leave for 3 minutes then stir in the vanilla essence.

5 Use the wooden spoon to beat the mixture until it darkens in colour, and becomes thicker and granular in texture. Pour into a well-oiled tray (use the bowl scraper to get all the toffee out of the pan).

6 Leave to cool for about 15 minutes. Oil the knife and use it to mark the toffee into squares.

7 When the toffee is cold it will break easily into squares. Store in an airtight tin.

8 Traditionally, a walnut half was placed in the centre of each square of toffee. You can do this, leave it plain or put something more interesting on top – you choose!

Gundy

Sir Walter Scott wrote that he remembered Gundy being sold by Mrs Flockart in the Potter Row in Edinburgh when he was a boy.

Adv

45 mins

Cook

Hob

Have Ready

450g (1lb) soft brown sugar

1 dessertspoon golden syrup or treacle

50g (2oz) butter

few drops of aniseed or cinnamon oil

strong soup pot

baking tray, oiled *(see page 7)*

wooden spoon

dessertspoon

teaspoon

teacup

To Make

1. Put the butter, sugar and syrup or treacle into the pan and stir over a medium heat until the ingredients are dissolved. Bring the mixture to the boil.
2. Turn down the heat until the mixture is just boiling. Leave the wooden spoon in the pan to stop the mixture from boiling over and stir occasionally to prevent sticking and burning. Boil for 20 minutes – keep watching it.
3. Test after 20 minutes: if the Gundy forms a hard ball in the foot of the cup it is ready. If it is still soft, continue to boil and test every 3 to 4 minutes until it forms a hard ball.
4. Turn off the heat. Leave to rest for 2 minutes and then stir in the flavouring you have chosen.
5. Quickly and carefully pour it into the oiled baking tray and leave to set. Oil the knife and use it to mark the warm toffee into squares.
6. When the Gundy is cold, tap it with a wooden spoon to break it into squares. Store in an airtight tin. Gundy takes a lot of sucking – it will keep you quiet for a long time!
7. You can make Toffee Apples while the toffee is still hot. Push a wooden stick into a clean apple and dip it into the toffee in the pan. Leave on a piece of greaseproof paper to cool. Toffee Apples are best eaten the day they are made.

Peppermint Creams

*Peppermint Creams were a great favourite with our great-grandparents. They are very simple to make – perhaps you could make them to surprise **your** grandparents!*

Simple

Needs left overnight

30 mins

No Cook ☒

Have Ready

- 1 egg white from a large egg or 2 egg whites from small eggs
- 225g (8oz) icing sugar
- peppermint essence or peppermint oil

- mixing bowl
- fork
- wooden spoon
- rolling pin
- sieve
- tablespoon
- plate
- non-stick baking parchment or greaseproof paper
- small cutter – any shape
- clean tea towel
- small paper cases

To Make

1. Separate the egg white from the yolk (see page 10) and put the egg white into the mixing bowl. Beat with the fork.
2. Place the sieve over the mixing bowl and sieve in 175g (6oz) icing sugar.
3. Mix well with the wooden spoon and gradually sieve in more icing sugar, half a tablespoonful at a time, until you have a stiff paste.
4. Shake a little icing sugar on to the worktop, then scrape the paste out on to the icing sugar.
5. Add 3 or 4 drops of peppermint essence or oil and gently knead it all together with your fingers until the paste is smooth. Taste a small piece of the paste – if the peppermint flavour is not strong enough, add 1 or 2 more drops of flavouring.
6. Rub some icing sugar on the rolling pin and roll the paste out to 0.5cm (¼ inch). Cut into shapes.
7. Cut a piece of paper to cover the plate. Lay the peppermint shapes on top of the paper on the plate. Cover them with a clean tea towel and leave overnight in a cool place (not the fridge) to set.
8. Place in the small paper cases and store in an airtight container.

Simple

30 mins

No Cook ☒

Marzipan Dates

Dundee, on the east coast of Scotland, is a busy seaport. It used to be well known for the import of almonds. These are used in many dishes which are traditional to this area, particularly in sweets. Ground almonds are used to make marzipan. Here is a sweetie which is quick and easy to make as it needs no cooking at all. You can make plenty for yourself and your friends!

HAVE READY

225g (8oz) whole, pitted dates

225g (8oz) marzipan

110g (4oz) caster sugar

4 large plates

sharp knife

small paper cases

TO MAKE

1 Lay the dates on a plate and gently open them with the knife.

2 Put the caster sugar on another plate.

3 Place the marzipan on a plate and knead it with your hands until it is warm and soft.

4 Decide how much marzipan you'd like to have inside your dates and divide the marzipan into pieces with the knife.

5 Take a piece of marzipan in your hands and shape it into a roll the length of a date.

6 Place the roll of marzipan in the centre of a date, then close the date so you have a 'date sandwich' with yellow marzipan in the middle.

7 Roll the filled date in the caster sugar and lay it on the empty plate.

8 Repeat steps 5 to 7 until the marzipan is finished. If there are any dates left over, chop them up add some grated cheese and put inside two pieces of bread – a healthy, tasty snack to try!

9 Place the Marzipan Dates in the paper cases. Store in an airtight container – how long can you keep them in there, I wonder?

The Baxter Story

The Baxter family business was born 128 years ago in a little grocery shop on Spey Street, Fochabers – George Baxter's. The grocer's wife, Margaret, made some strawberry jam in the back shop. It was good jam. George asked her to make more for him to sell in his front shop. Margaret's jams became very popular with the villagers, the local gentry and the ladies from many of the villages around Speyside.

In due course, George's eldest son, William, joined the business and opened the village store's wholesale department. On his bicycle, armed with his samples, he went to offer jams made to his mother's delicious recipes, to other shops in distant corners of the country. Later, tea, coffee and many other grocery products were added to Willie Baxter's sales list.

In 1914, William and his wife, Ethel, who was also a very keen cook, decided to build a new factory across the river from Fochabers with local stone, and the roof timbers came from a cargo ship which had been washed ashore on a local beach. The fertile soils of Moray provided the small factory with marvellous fruit and vegetables, and from the surrounding hills and glens came the freshest of game. In 1929, Ethel produced Royal Game Soup,

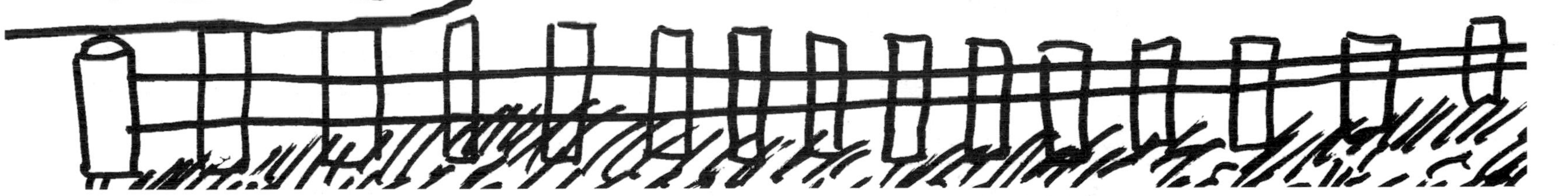

which was to become known all over the world and today is one of the world's best-selling quality soups. This was the beginning of Baxter's current family of fine foods.

The next generation, Gordon and Ian, continued in their parent's footsteps by working together to make the Baxter business the success story it is today. After the last war, Gordon and Ian returned to a business employing only 11 people of the original 35. It was very hard work, but they were determined to build the business and to base it on quality products, using traditional, wholesome ingredients, such as could be found in their mother's Royal Game Soup. Gordon's wife, Ena, too, has played a major role in the development of Baxters of Speyside, creating new recipes and cooking on television.

Today, Gordon and Ena's children, the fourth generation, are actively involved in the running of this still very independent, family-owned company. Audrey, Andrew and Michael continue in the commitment and dedication to being the best in the field and to seeing their own children become part of the wider Baxter story.

Bibliography

Recommended reading for more adventurous recipes and for further information on Scottish traditional cooking

Brown, Catherine, *Scottish Regional Recipes* (Penguin)
Brown, Catherine, *Broths to Bannocks* (John Murray)
Clark, Lady, *The Cookery Book of Lady Clark of Tillypronie* (Southover Press)
Fitzgibbon, Theodora, *Traditional Scottish Cookery* (Fontana)
Fitzgibbon, Theodora, *A Taste of Scotland* (Pan)
The Glasgow Cookery Book (John Smith)
Graham, Angus, *Skipness: Memoirs of a Highland Estate* (Canongate Academic)
Johnson, S. and J. Boswell, *A Journey to the Western Islands of Scotland* (Penguin)
Kirk, E. W., *Tried Favourites Cookery Book* (Johnston, and Horace Marshall & Son)
MacLaren, Kate, M., *Mrs MacLaren's Cookery Book* (Moray & Nairn Newspaper Co.)
McNeill, Marian, F., *The Scots Kitchen* (Blackie & Son)
McNeill, Marian, F., *The Scots Cellar* (Lochar Publishing)
Memoirs of a Highland Lady, 1797–1827, (John Murray)

Index

Aberdeen Crulla, 48
Aberdeen Date Scones, 30

Balmoral Shortbread, 57
Bannock, Pitcaithly, 62
Bannocks, Fife, 40
Baps (Scots Breakfast Rolls), 34
Baps, Breakfast (without yeast), 38
Barley Water, 92
Bere Bannocks (Barley Bannocks), 18
Berwickshire Fruit Loaf, 90
Black Bun, 88
Black Piece, 75
Blackcurrant Drink, Quick, 98
Blaeberry Jam, 101
Bonnach Imeach, 41
Border Tart, 64
Bramble and Rosehip Jam, 106
Bread (without yeast), 37
Bride's Bonn (Bridal Cake), 29
Broonie, Orkney, 72
Brunnies, 25
Butteries (Buttery Rowies), 32
Buttermilk Bread, 36

Canmore Buns, 46
Cheugh Jeans (Glasgow Toffee), 119

Date Scones, Aberdeen, 30
Dreaming Bread (Story of), 55
Dropped Scones, 26
Dundee Cake, 86

Ecclefechan Butter Tart, 67
Edinburgh Gingerbread, 76
Edinburgh Tart (Queen Mary's Tart), 68
Eyemouth Tart, 66

Famous Scottish Sweeties (Story of), 120
Fatty Cutties, 20
Fife Bannocks, 40
Fochabers Gingerbread, 73
Fruit Loaf, Berwickshire, 90

Glasgow Toffee (Cheugh Jeans), 119
Granny's Loaf, 85
Gundy, 122

Helensburgh Tablet, 121

Inverness Gingerbread, 71

Lemon Cheese (Lemon Curd), 116
Lemonade, Old Fashioned, 93

Marmalade, Breakfast Orange, 114
Marmalade Jelly, 110
Marmalade, Poor Man's, 113
Marzipan Dates, 124
Mashlum Scones, 17
Matrimony Jam, 105
Mealie Bannocks, 28
Melting Moments, 50
Mrs MacLaren's Gingerbread, 74
Mrs McNab's Scones, 22

Oat Shortbread, 56
Oatcakes, Traditional Highland, 42
Oatmeal Cakes, 44
Orange Jelly, 112
Orange Marmalade, Breakfast, 114
Orkney Broonie, 72

Parlies, 70
Peppermint Creams, 123
Petticoat Tails, 58
Pitcaithly Bannock, 62
Poor Man's Marmalade, 113
Potato Scones, 21

Queen Mary's Tart (Edinburgh Tart), 68

Raspberry Jam, 108
Raspberry Vinegar, 94
Rolls, Scots Breakfast (Baps), 34
Rosehip and Bramble Jam, 106
Rosehip Jelly, 102
Rowan Jelly, 104
Rowies, Aberdeen (Butteries), 32

Sair Heidies, 47
Scots Breakfast Rolls (Baps), 34
Seed Cake, Scots, 78
Selkirk Bannock, 82
Shortbread, Simple, 54
Shortbread, Traditional Plain Scots, 52
Snow Cake, 79
Soda Scones, 16
Sour Skons, 24
Strawberry Jam, Wild, 109
Strawberry Sandwich, Scottish, 80
Stokos, 96
Stoorum, 97

Tablet, Helensburgh, 121
Tantallon Cakes, 60
Tattie Scones, 21
Toffee, Glasgow Toffee (Cheugh Jeans), 119
Gundy, 122
Traditional Scottish Breads (Story of), 27

Vinegar Cake, 84

Wheaten Breads (Story of), 23